New Directions for
Adult and Continuing
Education

Susan Imel
Jovita M. Ross-Gordon
COEDITORS-IN-CHIEF

Learning Transfer in Adult Education

Leann M. R. Kaiser
Karen Kaminski
Jeffrey M. Foley
EDITORS

Number 137 • Spring 2013
Jossey-Bass
San Francisco

Learning Transfer in Adult Education
Leann M. R. Kaiser, Karen Kaminski, Jeffrey M. Foley (eds.)
New Directions for Adult and Continuing Education, no. 137
Susan Imel, Jovita M. Ross-Gordon, Coeditors-in-Chief

Microfilm copies of issues and articles are available in 16mm and 35mm, as well as microfiche in 105mm, through University Microfilms Inc., 300 North Zeeb Road, Ann Arbor, Michigan 48106-1346.

NEW DIRECTIONS FOR ADULT AND CONTINUING EDUCATION (ISSN 1052-2891, electronic ISSN 1536-0717) is part of The Jossey-Bass Higher and Adult Education Series and is published quarterly by Wiley Subscription Services, Inc., A Wiley Company, at Jossey-Bass, One Montgomery Street, Suite 1200, San Francisco, CA 94104-4594. Periodicals Postage Paid at San Francisco, California, and at additional mailing offices. POSTMASTER: Send address changes to New Directions for Adult and Continuing Education, Jossey-Bass, One Montgomery Street, Suite 1200, San Francisco, CA 94104-4594

New Directions for Adult and Continuing Education is indexed in CIJE: Current Index to Journals in Education (ERIC); Contents Pages in Education (T&F); ERIC Database (Education Resources Information Center); Higher Education Abstracts (Claremont Graduate University); and Sociological Abstracts (CSA/CIG).

INDIVIDUAL SUBSCRIPTION RATE (in USD): $89 per year US/Can/Mex, $113 rest of world; institutional subscription rate: $292 US, $332 Can/Mex, $366 rest of world. Single copy rate: $29. Electronic only–all regions: $89 individual, $292 institutional; Print & Electronic–US: $98 individual, $335 institutional; Print & Electronic–Canada/Mexico: $98 individual, $375 institutional; Print & Electronic–Rest of World: $122 individual, $409 institutional.

EDITORIAL CORRESPONDENCE should be sent to the Coeditors-in-Chief, Susan Imel, ERIC/ACVE, 1900 Kenny Road, Columbus, Ohio 43210-1090, e-mail: imel.l@osu.edu; or Jovita M. Ross-Gordon, Southwest Texas State University, EAPS Dept., 601 University Drive, San Marcos, TX 78666.

Cover photograph by Jack Hollingsworth@Photodisc

www.josseybass.com

CONTENTS

EDITORS' NOTES   1
Leann M. R. Kaiser, Karen Kaminski, Jeffrey M. Foley

1. Learning Transfer and Its Intentionality in Adult and   5
Continuing Education
Jeffrey M. Foley, Leann M. R. Kaiser
While transfer of learning is the ultimate goal of any instructional setting,
adult educators have few resources they can rely on to support planning
for transfer. This chapter offers an introduction to the concept of learning
transfer and initial ideas for building this into our educational practices.

2. Leveraging Experiential Learning Techniques for Transfer   17
Nate Furman, Jim Sibthorp
This chapter describes how experiential learning techniques can be
helpful in encouraging learning transfer as these techniques can foster a
depth of learning and cognitive recall necessary for transfer.

3. Problem-Based Learning: A Learning Environment for   27
Enhancing Learning Transfer
Woei Hung
Problem-based learning helps students make connections between
theory and real-world application. This chapter provides practical
methods for using problem-based learning to enhance the likelihood
of learning transfer.

4. Considering Components, Types, and Degrees of Authenticity   39
in Designing Technology to Support Transfer
Patricia L. Hardré
This chapter discusses the concept of authenticity in relation to using
technology to enhance learning and support transfer.

5. Brain-Friendly Teaching Supports Learning Transfer   49
Jacqueline McGinty, Jean Radin, Karen Kaminski
The authors present the workings of the human brain and how this
knowledge can be used to create brain-friendly learning environments
that support transfer of learning.

6. Racial and Cultural Factors and Learning Transfer   61
Rosemary Closson
This chapter addresses the potential influence of including ethnicity or culture as a
variable in the learning transfer process.

7. Understanding Transfer as Personal Change: Concerns,   71
Intentions, and Resistance
Jeani C. Young
Personal change stemming from learning experiences is the focus of this chapter.
Models of change and transition are used to explain the occurrence of and resistance
to transfer.

8. Applying Transfer in Practice   83
Karen Kaminski, Jeffrey M. Foley, Leann M. R. Kaiser
The authors offer a synthesis of the ideas presented in previous chapters by encour-
aging an application of learning transfer to adult learning settings.

Index   91

Editors' Notes

Learning transfer, simply stated, is the ability of a learner to apply skills and knowledge learned in one situation or setting to another (Cormier & Hagman, 1987; Thomas, 2007). This is the ultimate goal of participating in a workshop, class, or other educational pursuit. The learner should be able to effectively use the knowledge or skills gained in these educational settings at work, at home, or in the community (Broad, 1997). If transfer of learning is consciously included in our design and facilitation of learning, we have an enhanced likelihood of attaining this key education tenet.

The topic of learning transfer is not new. In fact, there is a solid body of research examining practices that lead to learning transfer in the contexts of education, training, and human resource development (Baldwin & Ford, 1988; Ford & Weissbein, 1997; Holton & Baldwin, 2003; Holton, Bates, & Rouna, 2000; Sousa, 2011). While there is a strong understanding of how to support transfer of learning within formal education and job settings, few other adult education settings account for learning transfer in the planning or implementation of their educational programs (Merriam & Leahy, 2005). This means we have little evidence that what is taught in one setting or situation is transferred to another, or how to achieve this goal. This issue is an attempt to add depth to the body of knowledge that informs learning transfer in adult education.

It is our hope that this issue can assist practitioners in a wide variety of adult education settings to define what learning transfer means in their area of focus. In addition, they will understand the importance of design for transfer and be encouraged to apply techniques to improve learning transfer for their learners. To achieve this purpose, each chapter included in this issue will introduce and expand upon transfer of learning from a particular focus area.

In Chapter 1, Jeffrey M. Foley and Leann M. R. Kaiser offer an introduction to the concept of learning transfer. They also discuss tools that are central to the context of learning transfer. These ideas are foundational to many of the subsequent chapters in the issue; thus, we would suggest beginning this issue by reading this chapter.

In Chapter 2, Nate Furman and Jim Sibthorp begin the discussion of understanding learning transfer through a specific lens: experiential learning. They highlight how common experiential learning techniques such as service learning and project-based learning can be used to encourage transfer of learning. In addition, they include three adult learning examples that explain how experiential learning techniques can be integrated to optimize transfer of learning.

NEW DIRECTIONS FOR ADULT AND CONTINUING EDUCATION, no. 137, Spring 2013 © 2013 Wiley Periodicals, Inc.
Published online in Wiley Online Library (wileyonlinelibrary.com) • DOI: 10.1002/ace.20039

In Chapter 3, Woei Hung approaches learning transfer from the perspective of problem-based learning. The chapter begins with a discussion on why students may fail to transfer learning and the role that problem-solving skills play. He proposes that problem-based learning may address these issues and shares design guidelines for using problem-based learning to enhance learning transfer.

In Chapter 4, Patricia L. Hardré focuses on the concept of authenticity and discusses how this is a key for using technology for instruction in ways that enhance and support learning transfer. She discusses how an authentic technology representation shows learners what a task, context, or experience will be like in real practice, lending to a greater likelihood of learning transfer.

In Chapter 5, Jacqueline McGinty, Jean Radin, and Karen Kaminski discuss cognitive learning theory and its relationship to learning transfer. To demonstrate this link, the authors present examples of learning environments and instruction facilitation techniques that are compatible with the brain's natural processes, using the concept of brain-based teaching.

In Chapter 6, Rosemary Closson begins by noting that infrequently has race, ethnicity, or culture been included as a variable when explaining the learning transfer process. She continues by exploring available theoretical and anecdotal evidence for how these factors may influence learning transfer, concluding the chapter with suggestions for practitioners.

In Chapter 7, Jeani C. Young explores the idea that transfer equals personal change. She introduces models of change that help describe, support, and predict the transfer that may or may not occur through participation in adult learning experiences. Understanding transfer as not only the application of knowledge in a different context but as a path to personal change is discussed.

In Chapter 8, Karen Kaminski, Jeffrey M. Foley, and Leann M. R. Kaiser encourage readers of this issue to choose one or more of the focus areas presented in Chapters 2 through 7 and synthesize the information for use in their own adult education setting. The authors walk the readers through a process of transfer and within that how to apply instructional design techniques to increase intentional planning for learning transfer.

We would encourage all readers to approach this issue of *New Directions for Adult and Continuing Education* by first reading Chapter 1. This chapter will give an overview of the foundational ideas related to learning transfer, which are pertinent to understanding subsequent chapters. Then, choose to read any of the additional chapter(s) that are relevant and of interest. Finally, to assist in creating a practical plan to support learning transfer in your own education practices, Chapter 8 is a good chapter with which to conclude reading this issue.

It is our hope that each reader of this issue will understand that "education can achieve abundant transfer if it is designed to do so" (Perkins & Salomon, 1992, Teaching for Transfer section, para. 6).

Leann M. R. Kaiser
Karen Kaminski
Jeffrey M. Foley
Editors

References

Baldwin, T. T., & Ford, J. K. (1988). Transfer of training: A review and direction for research. *Personnel Psychology, 41*, 63–105.
Broad, M. L. (1997). Transfer concepts and research overview. In M. L. Broad (Ed.), *Transferring learning to the workplace* (pp. 1–18). Alexandria, VA: American Society for Training and Development.
Cormier, S. M., & Hagman, J. D. (1987). *Transfer of learning: Contemporary research and applications*. San Diego, CA: Academic Press.
Ford, K. J., & Weissbein, D. A. (1997). Transfer of learning: An updated review and analysis. *Performance Improvement Quarterly, 10*(2), 22–41.
Holton, E. F., & Baldwin, T. T. (2003). *Improving learning transfer in organizations*. San Francisco, CA: Jossey-Bass.
Holton, E. F., Bates, R. A., & Rouna, W. E. A. (2000). Development of a generalized learning transfer system inventory. *Human Resource Development Quarterly, 11*(4), 333–360.
Merriam, S. B., & Leahy, B. (2005). Learning transfer: A review of the research in adult education and training. *PAACE Journal of Lifelong Learning, 14*, 1–24.
Perkins, D. N., & Salomon, G. (1992). Transfer of learning. In T. Husen & T. Postlethwaite (Eds.), *The international encyclopedia of education* (2nd ed). Oxford, England: Pergamon Press. Retrieved from http://learnweb.harvard.edu/alps/thinking/docs/traencyn.htm
Sousa, D. A. (2011). *How the brain learns* (4th ed.). Thousand Oaks, CA: Corwin.
Thomas, E. (2007). Thoughtful planning fosters learning transfer. *Adult Learning, 18*(3–4), 4–8.

LEANN M. R. KAISER is an assistant professor in the Adult Education and Training Program at Colorado State University.

KAREN KAMINSKI is the chair of the Master of Education in Adult Education and Training in the School of Education at Colorado State University.

JEFFREY M. FOLEY is an assistant professor in the Adult Education and Training Program at Colorado State University.

1

This chapter offers an introduction to learning transfer and the major concepts related to this topic. Encouraging the intentional use of learning transfer in adult and continuing education settings is emphasized.

Learning Transfer and Its Intentionality in Adult and Continuing Education

Jeffrey M. Foley, Leann M. R. Kaiser

What Is Learning Transfer in Adult Education?

Three unemployed adults sign up for a back-to-work course at their local workforce education center. The course is designed to cover quite a bit of information in a series of classes spanning 3 weeks such as resume writing, completing electronic applications, interview skills, and other job-hunting skills. The instructor is well versed in workforce theory and has facilitated this course many times. To ensure that the participants have the information they need to successfully find employment, the instructor has put many hours into PowerPoint slides, handouts, and other job-searching resources. The course went quite well, and the end survey sheets indicate that learners "gained a lot from the course."

Each of the learners in this course was motivated to attend and is eager to gain employment. After the course, Sue's head is spinning; there was so much information that she is finding she is spending a lot of time going back through the handouts. Bob, however, feels like he absorbed all of the information, yet he is having a very difficult time figuring out where to start and how to proceed. Alice attended the course a few times before and has a high level of mastery over the skills she needs to move forward—her challenge is finding the confidence to implement the right set of actions to secure a job.

These learners had a good experience in this course, and the instructor had sincere intentions of helping the learners prepare to gain employment. The disconnect is that the instructor did not design the instruction with learning transfer in mind. If the instructor had implemented specific instructional

NEW DIRECTIONS FOR ADULT AND CONTINUING EDUCATION, no. 137, Spring 2013 © 2013 Wiley Periodicals, Inc.
Published online in Wiley Online Library (wileyonlinelibrary.com) • DOI: 10.1002/ace.20040

strategies that focus on learning transfer into the course design, the learner should leave the course with a greater likelihood of applying the new knowledge and skills to help him or her attain a job. This issue of *New Directions for Adult and Continuing Education* focuses on how to design instruction to enhance learning transfer in adult education and training settings.

Broad (1997) defined learning transfer as the "effective and continuing application by learners—to their performance of jobs or other individual, organizational, or community responsibilities—of knowledge and skills gained in the learning activities" (p. 2). Merriam and Leahy (2005) reviewed the available empirical studies in adult education and learning transfer from 1990 to 2005, noting that much of it came from human resource development and training areas. Within the research they reviewed, the focus was generally on the transfer of a skill, learned in school or work training, to the workplace. Although narrow, this research focus is not surprising. These are settings in which a return on investment of the time, energy, and financial resources dedicated to training is key to both the success of the business and the continuation of training programs. Thus, the vast array of other adult learning settings to which the learning may be transferred has not been well documented in the literature. On a practical level, this also means that few adult education and training programs account for transfer (Merriam & Leahy, 2005). Yet there is a strong need to foster learning transfer in all areas of adult learning such as work skills, life skills, adult literacy, and English as a second language (ESL), just to name a few examples. Think for a moment about a course, seminar, or training that you facilitate. In this context, what measures do you take to ensure that transfer occurs? Asking this critically reflective question is the key to designing learning for transfer.

An additional implication, stemming from the fact that most of our knowledge about adult learning transfer originates in workplace training literature, is that the research does not discuss in any depth the ways that learning transfer also applies to, and among, school, community, family, and life situations. There are myriad combinations of where or when learning may occur and to where it might be transferred. The scenario many people would think of first is learning a skill in the classroom and then being able to use that at work or at home. But learning transfer in adult education extends far beyond this. For example, an informal learning situation such as gathering information on gardening from a web site to grow vegetables might result in this same individual's transferring that knowledge to also grow flowers. Or perhaps a nonformal ESL course allows the learner not only to pass an exam at the end of the course but also to communicate in a grocery store. We know that adult education finds its home far beyond the formal classroom, and this is also the case for learning transfer. Thus, learning transfer is not only a good idea to keep in mind when designing and facilitating adult learning; it is also fundamentally tied to all adult learning. Calais (2006) stated this relationship well by noting that we are always working toward transfer of learning because "we constantly perceive and interpret new things in light of our past experience" (p. 6).

Models of Transfer

Various distinctions in learning transfer have been discussed in the literature. Included here is a brief overview of several of the major concepts.

Near and Far Transfer. *Near transfer* refers to when a new situation is closely similar to the original learning situation. Near transfer usually includes specific concepts and skills such as learning to drive a car and then using those same skills to drive a truck. Conversely, in *far transfer* the original and new situations are dissimilar. The learner may not automatically understand the connection between the two situations (Detterman, 1993). As an example of far transfer, a student may learn math skills and then use the problem-solving skills fundamental to that math to design an electrical circuit.

High- and Low-Road Transfer. Perkins and Salomon (1989) argued that while near and far transfers do occur, far transfer does not occur as readily for many students. Simply understanding the idea of far transfer itself does not give a facilitator the tools to teach for far transfer. Thus, Perkins and Salomon introduced low-road and high-road transfer. In low-road transfer, a skill is well practiced in a learning setting and a learner can replicate it when the circumstances are similar to the original learning context. The replication occurs in a reflexive and automatic manner. High-road transfer involves more assistance for a learner to be able to reflectively think about what was learned and then deliberately abstract from the original context to connect it to other contexts. This assistance may take the form of encouraging cognitive understanding, purposeful and conscious analysis, mindfulness, and application of strategies across disciplines. High-road transfer is not dependent on identifying superficial similarities, but rather understanding deeper analogies.

Positive and Negative Transfer. We are always interpreting our current experience in light of our previous experiences. This can affect learning transfer in two ways. With positive transfer, learning from a previous context complements a current context. In other words, the experiences from both are complementary and in agreement. In negative transfer, previous experiences interfere with learning and transfer into a new context. When negative transfer occurs, a person is unable or unwilling to see how learning might be used in another context because of contrary experiences, expectations, or connotations between the two (Leberman, McDonald, & Doyle, 2006). For example, a person may have learned Spanish, but that knowledge may confuse the same person when he or she is trying to learn German.

Haskell's Taxonomies for Transfer of Learning. Calais (2006) described a slightly different way of categorizing learning transfer rather than the dual classifications previously used. Calais used Haskell's Taxonomy, which includes six progressive levels of learning transfer: nonspecific, application, context, near, far, and displacement/creative. Calais argued that only the near, far, and displacement/creative levels require something new to be learned, and thus may result in transfer. Calais continued by stating that there are not only levels of transfer but different kinds of transfer. The first kind is based on types of knowledge (for example, declarative, procedural, or theoretical). The second kind is based on types of transfer, including content-to-content transfer, vertical transfer, and relational transfer. Haskell's Taxonomy is complex and not the focus of this chapter, but for more details, refer to Haskell (2001).

Barriers to Learning Transfer

Learning transfer may be a basic assumed outcome of most, if not all, learning situations. Educators want learners to be able to use knowledge or skills gained under their guidance in other situations. Even an individual engaged in learning without a facilitator most likely intends to take something forward from that learning.

While understanding the importance of learning transfer is not a point that needs to be belabored, it is imperative to understand that simply taking part in a learning transaction does not guarantee that the expectation of transfer will occur (refer to the scenario at the beginning of this chapter). In fact, each chapter in this issue examines different situations and methods through which the likelihood of learning transfer can be enhanced for adult learners. Thus, before these ideas on achieving transfer are explored, it is important to understand some of the potential barriers to learning transfer.

Thomas (2007) noted that barriers to transfer can be encountered before, during, and after the learning experience. A lack of foundational knowledge upon entering a learning situation, a lack of motivation or confidence during the learning, and a lack of support afterward can all adversely affect transfer. Lightner, Benander, and Kramer (2008) continued the discussion on barriers by noting that common classroom practices may not facilitate transfer. These include the facilitator's not modeling, rewarding, encouraging, or giving opportunities to express and practice transfer. Lightner et al. also discussed that facilitators who assume the learner needs to take on the responsibility to achieve transfer find less success in transfer occurring. An example might include a facilitator who does not demonstrate that the computer skills a learner gains to increase workplace proficiency can also be used to communicate with family or plan a budget.

Illeris (2009) argued that learning transfer difficulties often occur across learning space boundaries, for example, when something learned in school needs to be transferred to the workplace. He noted that integration projects between learning spaces are important to encourage transfer. Illeris also asserted that the "transferability of different kinds of learning processes and learning outcomes appears as directly dependent on the type of learning (cumulative, assimilative, accommodative, or transformative) and the resulting knowledge" (p. 144). Thus, it is important to develop learning activities that encourage all four learning types. (For a further explanation of the learning types, see Illeris, 2009). Hager and Hodkinson (2009) continued this line of thinking by proposing that we should go as far as abandoning the term *learning transfer* and "think instead of learning as becoming within a transitional process of boundary crossing" (p. 635). They argued that these boundaries are not just between school and work but other areas such as parenthood and retirement.

Finally, one of the most basic barriers to transfer is overlooking it in both design and facilitation phases. Simply ignoring that transfer needs to be accounted for, and that it may not occur on its own, is a common but costly mistake. This idea will be further addressed in the subsequent chapters in this issue.

General Tools to Improve Learning Transfer

Increasing learning transfer essentially entails integrating effective processes and methods of instruction into daily practice. Strategies such as scaffolding, schema theory, purposeful reflection, repetition, concept mapping, and utilizing a diversity of instructional methods increase learning transfer (Ford & Weissbein, 1997). Often, the challenge is determining where to integrate these tools into instruction when facilitators are already so bound for time, resources, and energy. The critically reflective facilitator of learning will not attempt to "add" these tools to instruction but actually replace less effective tools with more effective ones.

Scaffolding. Picture a little girl learning how to ride a bike. If she is given a bike and told to go ride, any number of outcomes are possible. However, if the girl is provided safety equipment, training wheels, support, and encouragement, the structures are in place to help the girl master the goal of riding a bike. As the girl practices, she finds that the training wheels are cumbersome and are keeping her from riding in a way that she wants. The training wheels can be taken off and the next step to learning can take place. If this step does not work, the training wheels can be put back on until the girl is more comfortable with the feel of the bike. In the end, the girl discovers that with some confidence and muscle mastery she can ride anywhere she wants without the additional supporting structures that were once necessary. While this is a simplistic example of scaffolding a learning experience to best ensure mastery of a given learning goal, it is an experience many are familiar with and is easily relatable.

Scaffolding a learning experience is a combination of ensuring that the learning environment, instructional plan, supporting resources, and instructional delivery are structured in a manner that best supports learning. Scaffolding in construction helps support the building process. The scaffolding does not actually build the building, the worker does. The scaffolding is just a temporary tool that assists the worker in the construction process. So is instructional scaffolding just a temporary tool that assists the learner in the process of constructing knowledge. The art of facilitating learning is to provide the necessary structure and support to assist the learner in constructing his or her own way of knowing.

Scaffolding can take on many forms of support. In the simplest terms, the facilitator of learning wants to ensure that the learning environment is a safe and energetic place for learning to occur. Being conscious that the setup of the room, the temperature, the light, and the sound are significant physical factors of establishing a learning environment is important. The next level is emotional safety where specific attention is paid to inclusivity, language bias, and sociocultural diversity. Then there are the considerations of openness, communication style, and choice of instructional methods. While individually these forms of support may seem simple to control, in totality they have a large impact on the conductivity of the learning environment for learning and learning transfer.

More complex forms of scaffolding in the learning experience focus on authenticity. The written, audio, visual, and tactile resources introduced into the learning environment serve as scaffolding to support learning. The key to the effectiveness of the resource is relevance. The more relevant and authentic a learning resource is to the actual applied end use of the learning, the more impactful that resource will be to learning transfer. For example, a learner can be shown how to use a word processing program, but that does not automatically mean that he or she can then write a thesis. Even though the intent was to have the learner master a word processing program, the gap between the known (word processing program) and the unknown (writing a thesis) was too large for learning transfer to take place.

Another form of scaffolding pertains to community learning and problem-based learning. In community learning or group learning situations, the learners serve as the temporary support structure for each other in the learning process. In problem-based learning, the learners take on successively more difficult tasks or problems as they master the current challenge. Both of these learning methods are discussed in depth in the chapters in this issue.

In reading this information on scaffolding, the concern may arise that these are just good instructional methods, rather than directly relating to increasing learning transfer. This is one case where the absence of a phenomenon defines the outcome. Without scaffolding, the learner can spend a majority of the time devoted to learning just trying to develop a foundation and frame of reference for the learning. The time spent struggling to grasp specific concepts that could be supported by scaffolding instruction directly eats away at the time for the learning, mastery, and building toward learning transfer.

Schema. Schema is the concept that information is organized by the learner in specific patterns or order. Our schemas are changed or modified by our interaction with the world through sight, sound, taste, and communication. As we interact with a new phenomenon, we compare and contrast those phenomena with what we have previously experienced. Our current way of knowing and the foundation of how we interact with the world is often referred to as a worldview. Thus, schema is the foundation or fabric through which we form our worldview.

In its simplest form, schema is how we categorize information. If we consider our brain as an elaborate filing system, our schema is organized in drawers of similar information so that it is easier for us to recall information as well as to retain new information. If you see an animal that has four legs, a tail, and pointy ears, you brain quickly goes to the animal file drawer, sorts through and pulls out the file for "cat." Most people are familiar with the domestic house cat, but there are many types of cats, large and small, that all have these same features. When we see a different type of cat, we recognize it as a cat, learn what this new cat is—perhaps a lion—and add it to our file on cats and easily store it away. Good facilitators of transfer find ways to help learners activate (or find the file for) their existing schema that is related to the learning at hand. This increases the likelihood of retaining this new information for later application.

In a more complex example, picture an adult learner who finished his primary and secondary education 20 years ago. He experienced a very traditional form of education where the professor (*Latin*: person who professes) was the center of knowing and the deliverer of knowledge. This learner has held to this view of education for the entirety of his adulthood to date. Because of a recent layoff, this learner has decided to return to higher education in hopes of increasing his employability. When he enters the classroom for the first learning session, he is greeted by a facilitator who uses a collaborative and co-creating (constructivist) method of facilitating learning.

In this learner's current worldview, the role of the facilitator is to impart knowledge to the learner. The student's role is to take or absorb that knowledge and at some point prove to the facilitator that he or she has mastered the concepts. Yet in this current situation, the role of the facilitator is to serve as a facilitator of learning, create a safe and energized learning environment, and engage the learner(s) in the co-construction of new ways of knowing. The learner's role is to directly engage in the learning with the support of the facilitator.

This learner should be supported in making a modification to his worldview based on his current schema and the new information at hand. The question becomes: How can a facilitator provide the support and resources to assist a learner in making this modification? The chapters in this issue provide examples of how to support learners as they challenge their known schema and integrate new information into their worldview. When reading these chapters, try to keep the concept of schema as a mental frame through which to explore different approaches and methods to facilitating learning.

Purposeful Reflection. In a traditional teaching and learning paradigm, information is presented by the facilitator through lecture, PowerPoint, or other delivery techniques (Palmer, 2007). When the learning session is over the learners are left to interpret the meaning of the subject presented (or not). Purposeful reflection is a tool that can be introduced into instruction that helps the learner stay engaged with the subject and to start laying roots for meaningful transfer by creating relevance. The word *purposeful* is used as an indicator that this is a guided form of reflection and not just a general reflection on the subject.

Picture a facilitator who just delivered an energetic and engaging PowerPoint presentation that explored the roots and development of adult education. The facilitator has about 10 minutes left in class and asks the learners to take out a sheet of paper and answer this question: "In the context of the material presented in class, please think of an adult learning situation that you have participated in recently (another class, a training, etc.) and try to identify similarities and differences from your experience to one of the roots of adult education that was covered in the presentation." So instead of just asking, "Please reflect on the material presented today and summarize the main points" (which is a valid classroom assessment technique in itself), the facilitator is asking the learners to draw relevance between the subject covered and one of their life experiences. That is purposeful reflection.

Here are some suggestions for purposeful reflection:

- Attempt to tie real experiences to the presentation of theory or concepts.
- Allow for a pause between questions when facilitating a discussion.
- Encourage alternative solutions to problems presented and encourage different or dissenting viewpoints.
- Have three or four reflective activities at the ready for when you might need them.
- Use electronic discussion boards, blogs, and the like to encourage reflection and sharing outside of class.
- Make sure that reflections are directed toward achieving the stated learning outcomes.
- Use the reflective process to move toward higher levels of critical thinking as indicated in Bloom's taxonomy.
- Ask the learners to step out of their dominant worldview and experience the situation or problem through another's eyes.

Purposeful reflection is a powerful tool that enhances learning transfer in adult learning. The key to successful purposeful reflection is to be intentional in integrating this method into instruction and out-of-class assignments.

Repetition from Multiple Aspects. Repetition has been a long-standing tenet of education. Repetition is the revisiting of information at different points of time. From a cognitive theory perspective, the brain reinforces learning and strengthens neural pathway connections in part through repetition. While rote learning is memorization and recall of information without knowing the relevance, we recommend revisiting information from multiple aspects and different contexts to increase the likelihood of the learner making connections in his or her unique settings. Facilitating learning sessions that help the learner gain mastery of the new knowledge and skills increases the like-lihood of learning transfer.

Concept Mapping. Concept mapping is a tool that allows the learner to externalize a thought process or new information and then manipulate the individual pieces into a more cogent picture or flow process. Figure 1.1 is a concept map created for a research study.

The key elements of this concept map are the central theme, the major dependent and independent variables, and the sub-variables. This concept map might first appear to be very complex and difficult to interpret. But once learners are able to externalize all of the different variables, they can then start grouping and organizing the information into logical groups and then find the central theme (inductive reasoning). When facilitating the use of concept maps, the learner might start with a general theme and break the information into smaller parts or groups (deductive reasoning). Also, the learner can take one group of variables and move them from one side of the concept map to the other if that makes more sense. Concept mapping allows learners to organize, group, move, and reorganize information as they gain mastery over the information and the organizing process.

Diversity of Delivery Methods. Integrating a multitude of delivery methods into instruction can improve learning transfer. The brain loves stimulation. If facilitators find themselves falling back to the same delivery method for each class, they may find that their learning environment is becoming stale. A recent study (CDW-G, 2012) highlights that in the past two years half of higher education faculty report a shift away from the traditional lecture model, integrating group learning projects, self-paced study, virtual learning, and collaborative projects into their instruction. Some programs are moving to a flipped classroom where the lecture portion of the class is recorded so that the learner can access the information any time prior to the class via the Internet, and class time is devoted to interactive and experiential approaches to learning.

The ultimate goal is to identify what the learners need to best master the subject or content and choose the best methodology to engage those learners. This does not mean the death of traditional lecture, but allows the facilitator of learning to integrate lecture where it is the best tool to engage the learner in meeting the learning outcomes.

Learning Transfer: Revisiting Its Importance to Adult Learning

In this chapter, a cursory review of learning transfer, its role in adult learning, and the major models and tools related to the transfer of learning were discussed. The remainder of the chapters in this issue strive to add the necessary detail and context to this topic. For a facilitator practitioner involved in the

Figure 1.1. A Concept Map.

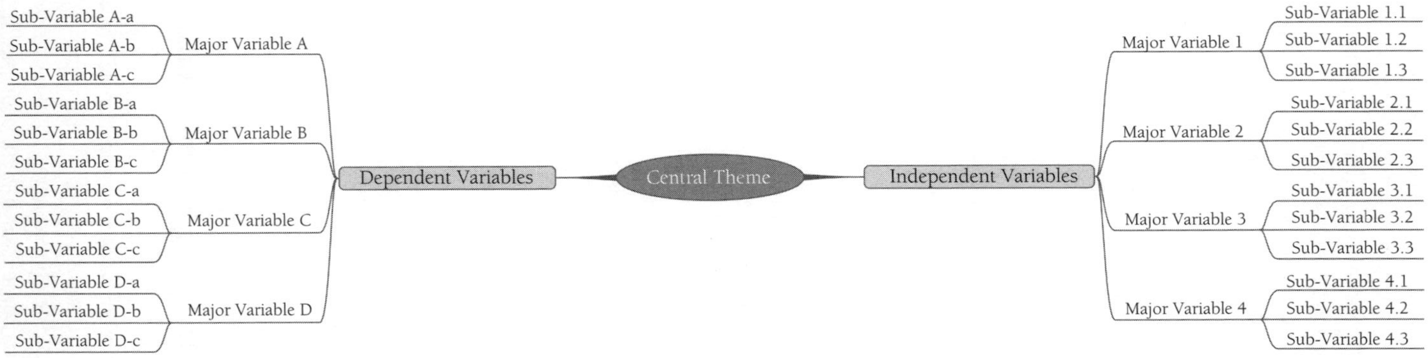

instructional design or facilitation process of adult learning, learning transfer is not an idea that can or should be ignored. This is not to suggest that practitioners do not want their learners to be able to take forward what they have learned and apply it in other situations. Rather, with few conversations happening around this topic, they may not have the available resources to achieve this goal. Thus, beginning with a foundation on learning transfer as shared here is an important starting place to encourage a greater awareness of the importance of planning for learning transfer in adult learning settings.

References

Broad, M. L. (1997). Transfer concepts and research overview. In M. L. Broad (Ed.), *Transferring learning to the workplace* (pp. 1–18). Alexandria, VA: American Society for Training and Development.

Calais, G. J. (2006). Haskell's taxonomies of transfer of learning: Implications for classroom instruction. *National Forum of Applied Educational Research Journal, 20*(3), 1–8.

CDW-G. (2012). *Learn now, lecture later.* Retrieved from http://newsroom.cdwg.com/features/feature-06-26-12.html

Detterman, D. K. (1993). The case for prosecution: Transfer as an epiphenomenona. In D. K. Detterman & R. J. Sternberg (Eds.), *Transfer on trial: Intelligence, cognition and instruction* (pp. 1–23). Norwood, NJ: Ablex.

Ford, J. K., & Weissbein, D. A. (1997). Transfer of training: An updated review and analysis. *Performance Improvement Quarterly, 10*(2), 22–41.

Hager, P., & Hodkinson, P. (2009). Moving beyond the metaphor of transfer of learning. *British Educational Research Journal, 35*(4), 619–638.

Haskell, E. H. (2001). *Transfer of learning: Cognition, instruction, and reasoning.* New York, NY: Academic Press.

Illeris, K. (2009). Transfer of learning in the learning society: How can the barriers between different learning spaces be surmounted and how can the gap between learning inside and outside schools be bridged? *International Journal of Lifelong Education, 28*(2), 137–148. doi: 10.1080/02601370902756986

Leberman, S., McDonald, L., & Doyle, S. (2006). *The transfer of learning: Participants' perspectives of adult education and training.* Burlington, VT: Gower.

Lightner, R., Benander, R., & Kramer, E. (2008). Faculty and student attitudes about transfer of learning. *InSight: A Journal of Scholarly Teaching, 3,* 58–66.

Merriam, S. B., & Leahy, B. (2005). Learning transfer: A review of the research in adult education and training. *PAACE Journal of Lifelong Learning, 14,* 1–24.

Palmer, P. J. (2007). *The courage to teach: Exploring the inner landscape of a teacher's life.* San Francisco, CA: Jossey-Bass.

Perkins, D. N., & Salomon, G. (1989). Rocky roads to transfer: Rethinking mechanisms of a neglected phenomenon. *Educational Psychologist, 24*(2), 113–142.

Thomas, E. (2007). Thoughtful planning fosters learning transfer. *Adult Learning, 18*(3–4), 4–8.

JEFFREY M. FOLEY is an assistant professor in the Adult Education and Training Program at Colorado State University.

LEANN M. R. KAISER is an assistant professor in the Adult Education and Training Program at Colorado State University.

New Directions for Adult and Continuing Education • DOI: 10.1002/ace

2

This chapter describes how experiential learning techniques such as service learning and problem-based learning can be leveraged to maximize transfer in adult populations. Specific examples of experiential learning in adult education programs are included.

Leveraging Experiential Learning Techniques for Transfer

Nate Furman, Jim Sibthorp

Adult education and training programs are diverse, ranging from learning computer languages to gaining teaching certifications to understanding digital photography to developing business acumen. These programs are characterized by the emphasis on using the skills learned after the end of the program, an idea commonly referred to as *learning transfer.* Learning transfer has been described "as the ultimate aim of teaching . . . however achieving this goal has been one of teaching's most formidable problems" (McKeough, Lupart, & Marini, 1995, p. vii) and is a hallmark of many adult education programs.

Experiential learning techniques can be helpful in fostering learning transfer. Techniques such as project-based learning, reflective learning, and cooperative learning provide authentic platforms for developing rich learning experiences. In contrast to more didactic forms of instruction, experiential learning techniques foster a depth of learning and cognitive recall necessary for transfer.

This chapter describes how experiential learning techniques can be used to encourage transfer of learning. First, we describe several of the key characteristics of experiential education and experiential learning. Second, we briefly summarize literature on learning transfer and experiential learning techniques. Third, we provide three examples of how experiential techniques may be integrated into adult education to optimize transfer in adult learning contexts. By the conclusion of the chapter, the reader will have a clear sense of how experiential techniques may be leveraged for transfer with adult learners.

New Directions for Adult and Continuing Education, no. 137, Spring 2013 © 2013 Wiley Periodicals, Inc.
Published online in Wiley Online Library (wileyonlinelibrary.com) • DOI: 10.1002/ace.20041

Experiential Education and Experiential Learning

Experiential education is a method of education informed by the philosophies of Dewey, the social constructivism of Vygotsky, and the developmental theories of Piaget (Roberts, 2011). As a discipline, experiential education places a premium on constructing individual meaning, honors the prior experience of students, and values ideals central to social change. As a practice, experiential education prioritizes active learning components, frequently uses reflection activities as a tool to develop further meaning, and emphasizes peer-to-peer interaction. Typically, it deemphasizes rote learning, memorization, and inflexible, didactic interactions between teacher and learner.

Experiential learning is not bound by the social milieu, traditions, or philosophies like experiential education is. It is often used to describe both "meaning making from theoretical knowledge *and* [emphasis added] nondirected informal life experience from formal education" (Fenwick, 2000, p. 243). Experiential learning structures include individual teaching techniques used by an instructor to achieve learning goals. For instance, an instructor may decide to design a *cooperative learning* project because that structure best develops student outcomes. Experiential learning may not require an instructor and may be as simple as someone teaching himself or herself to play the guitar or learn HTML code. There may be no direct, formal instruction of any sort, and the learner's ability to acquire the skill is largely determined by his or her own process of trial and error.

This chapter focuses on explicating the experiential learning techniques commonly used for educative purposes that are best aligned with learning transfer. Some specific examples of experiential techniques or methods of interest include the following.

Problem-Based Learning. This technique may use the students' interest in a problem to (a) create an experiment to answer a question or (b) develop a course of action that helps in resolving the problem (Haas & Furman, 2008). In agriculture, does rotating crops with nitrogen-fixating plants increase crop yield? Is it really colder at night on a north-facing slope? Students can answer these problems by designing rather simple experiments that actively engage them in the learning process instead of simply remembering the answers.

Project-Based Learning. Project-based learning takes the interests of the students and creates a project around those interests that is rich with educational content (Marienau & Reed, 2008; Thomas, 2000). For example, students may be interested in climbing a mountain. From an adventure recreation perspective, this could, in and of itself, be the goal. However, an experiential educator will readily see how this project can be used as an authentic platform for teaching a wide variety of topics, such as altitude, physics, judgment, safety, climbing, group dynamics, leadership, decision making, time management, planning, math, ecological zonation, environmental ethics, knots, and so on. The project has the capacity to make each of these content areas authentic.

New Directions for Adult and Continuing Education • DOI: 10.1002/ace

Cooperative Learning. This example deals with creating environments rich in learning between students, and where students learn from each other's perspectives and past experience (Hamm & Adams, 1992). This type of learning is readily evident in many distance learning programs, adult education programs, and continuing education programs where students learn through discourse, observation, and interaction with peers. One might readily notice that cooperative learning can be used in conjunction with other techniques.

Service Learning. Service learning combines educational objectives with community service needs (Bringle & Hatcher, 1996; Smith, 2008). The objectives and the service must be aligned in a way to benefit both the students and the community. A typical service-learning program might include some classroom sessions to prepare and situate a service experience, participation in a service experience, and a reflective component that links the lived experience and the education objective of the course or program. Such experiences can be used as ongoing features of a course or may be specifically aligned with a subset of the course content. If, for example, an educator uses an invasive species removal project in a context of learning about streamside restoration or biological encroachment, then the educational value becomes more rich and meaningful.

Reflective Learning. This concept allows students to make connections between theory and practice and allows the principles learned in a classroom to be applied elsewhere. Boyd and Fales (1983) describe reflective learning as "the process of internally examining and exploring an issue of concern, triggered by an experience, which creates and clarifies meaning in terms of self, and which results in a changed conceptual perspective" (p. 100). Reflective learning elements may include guided discussion, reflective writing exercises, blog writing, and essay-based examination.

These different types of experiential learning techniques—problem-based, project-based, cooperative, service, and reflective—are not entirely distinct from one another. Rather, they describe different ideas developed by different individuals and schools of thought at different times. Other ideas—such as collaborative learning, discovery learning, minimally guided learning, self-directed learning, and active learning—are also related. While these learning techniques maximize *depth* of learning and thinking and excel with process-focused educational content, they necessarily sacrifice *breadth*. Thus, experiential techniques may be considered less efficient methods of instruction for some learning outcomes such as content introduction or overview.

The five types of experiential learning techniques represent major approaches around which teachers might develop instruction. In addition to these ideas, educators may use a number of specific educational practices in their day-to-day lessons. Bonk and Cunningham (1998, pp. 33–34) provide examples of some of these practices:

- **Group processing and reflection.** Processing activities focus on both the individual and the group.

- **Social dialogue and elaboration.** Activities incorporate multiple solutions, novelty, uncertainty, and personal interests to encourage discourse.
- **Learning communities.** The classroom ethos supports "joint responsibility for learning, students are experts and have learning ownership, meaning is negotiated, and participation structures are understood and ritualized" (p. 34).
- **Assessment.** The focus on assessment is on the group as well as the individual, and the educational standards are socially negotiated.
- **Multiple viewpoints.** The instructor provides explanations, examples, and different ways of understanding problems.
- **Team choice and common interests.** Students are able to have choice in learning activities. Student and group autonomy, initiative, leadership, and active learning are encouraged.

Expanding on these ideas, Frontczak (1998) suggests that experiential learning is student-centered; that it emphasizes firsthand experience; that students are responsible for their own learning; that the orientation tilts toward flexibility and away from regimen; and that the goal of education includes a holistic combination of cognitive, affective, and behavioral processes.

Learning Transfer and Experiential Learning

Most of these experiential learning techniques and practices are well aligned with empirically supported approaches to teaching for transfer. Of specific note, reflection and processing information (Cranton, 2002; Jordi, 2010), active learning (Cox, 1997), discovery learning (Mayer & Wittrock, 1996), feedback plus remediation (Lee & Kahnweiler, 2000), and analogical approaches to thinking (Alexander & Murphy, 1999) are thought to enhance learning transfer. Reflection might include written, verbal, or strictly mental exercises designed to revisit covered course content and create additional mental connections. Active learning is generally considered more engaging and typically affords deeper interaction with the content, which itself is thought to increase transfer (Haskell, 2001). The provision of quality feedback coupled with reinforcement and remediation opportunities can be an effective way to enhance transfer potential (Lee & Kahnweiler, 2000). Drawing analogies between the course content and more distant applications can also assist with learning transfer, as the learner is more able to readily see the connections between the learning content and the application context. In addition, generally supported education principles such as goal setting and modeling are widely considered critical to andragogy, experiential learning, and learning transfer.

The recent work of Sibthorp, Furman, Paisley, Gookin, and Schumann (2011) adds to the existing literature on learning transfer in experiential programming. This study investigated how transfer operated in adults at an experiential education program run by the National Outdoor Leadership School (NOLS). Researchers asked alumni who completed NOLS courses 1 to 10 years previously about transfer, including what they learned from their program, if they transferred those skills, and what it was about the program that helped them transfer those skills to life post-course.

The study found support for several of the experiential learning techniques discussed in this chapter. Both time for practice and active learning were reported as important mechanisms that led to learning transfer. In addition, general educational approaches including modeling, goal setting, and overlearning (where students practice past the point of initial mastery) were reported as critical to learning transfer. Notably, however, some of the main experiential learning techniques that showed up in our study were not explicitly present in the extant literature.

For instance, research participants reported that instructors played a central role in mediating transfer through a variety of means, ranging from interpersonal support and personal inspiration to role modeling and the central means of instructional delivery. The specifics of the backcountry setting and course highlights were impactful. Course length and the sheer isolation this specific program afforded was an important catalyst for some types of learning. There was also learning potential in the group dynamics, which are likely more critical in a dense expeditionary setting than a typical classroom. While these are intentional practices on NOLS courses, they are also distinct to the nature and substance of an experiential outdoor education experience and its prolonged small group nature. Thus, these mechanisms are not universal but represent an important concept: that transfer mechanisms remain highly contextual in any type of educational setting. Table 2.1 summarizes the experiential learning techniques and exemplary quotes from research participants.

Another important aspect of this study was its focus on mechanisms of transfer beyond the direct influence of the program or educator. These mechanisms include the perceived value of the educational content, relevance to participants' occupation, and the opportunity to perform the skill post-program. These mechanisms of transfer—ones that are difficult to directly influence by an educational program—further illustrate the importance of the learner characteristics and the application context and climate. Although bound by specific contexts, this study illustrates ways that experiential learning can be incorporated into other programs to support the transfer of learning.

Integrating Experiential Techniques

As transfer techniques and mechanisms are context and content specific, three examples of generic programs are introduced next to illustrate how experiential learning techniques may be integrated into adult education. In addition, practices such as reflection, collaboration, feedback, goal setting, and choice

Table 2.1. Experiential Learning Techniques and Practices That Can Enhance Learning Transfer.

Experiential Learning Techniques	Exemplary Quote
Practice	"The instructors giving us freedom and the opportunity to lead and hike without them."
Active learning	"It's the style of learning that's most effective for me 'the big thing is to do it' is what NOLS managed (and what I needed)."
Content relevance	"The ability to get along with people is key to my success at work and in other aspects of my life."
Instructor: Support	"My instructors were my lifeline on the course. I felt comfortable asking them any question or problems I had and in turn they gave me their words of wisdom."
Instructor: Modeling	"The instructors were just great people and good role models."
Characteristics of the classroom	"The need . . . because of the real setting of the 'class-room.'"
Course highlight	"If it had not been for the day I climbed Wind River Peak. ... On this day, when I got to the top of the mountain, I realized in a really tangible way all I was capable of."
Course length	"Being isolated continuously for 75 days in a harsh environment."
Group dynamics	"If it had not been for the group conflict on my course, I probably would not have learned nearly as much about communication and openly accepting feedback, positive or constructive."

are encouraged as both good andragogy and transfer-enhancing instructional practices.

Program 1: English as a Second Language Course

- **Cooperative learning.** A course could incorporate a geography-based component where students observe physical, climate, economic, and political maps. Students work in pairs or small teams to create a labeled geographic model of a physical feature found on their map. This context-embedded lesson would address reading and writing objectives through active peer cooperation and collaboration.
- **Service learning.** A course could work with a state or community agency hoping to better provide services for nonnative English speakers. The students could work on translating material from English into their native language for use in brochures, web site, or other resources. Not only would this necessitate reading and writing, but also speaking and

communicating with the partner agency. Thus, while providing a service to the agency, the students are able to learn, practice, and reflect upon several course objectives around language use and interpretation.

- **Project-based learning.** This course could plan a tour of the local area. This project could involve research on potential sites and routes, correspondence and communication with destinations, making transportation and accommodation arrangements, and onsite interaction with English-speaking staff. Addressing a variety of listening, writing, and speaking objectives is possible.

Program 2: Online Personal Finance Course

- **Reflective learning.** This course could incorporate a reflective assignment that asks students to estimate what their net worth might be had they invested 10% of their lifelong income. This might be a very traumatizing assignment! It will require students to think reflectively on their financial decisions—and thus expose values—and then apply course content to predict what their investments might be in various investment forms.
- **Project-based learning.** This course could incorporate an investment strategy game where each student is asked to develop an imaginary investment portfolio and then measure gains and losses on a daily or weekly basis. Given the scope of the course, the instructor would likely be wise to constrain the choices in a meaningful way. This assignment would also provide opportunity to reflect on decisions and the processes that informed them.
- **Problem-based learning.** This course could incorporate a series of case studies, and each week a new case study is assigned. Each case study presents an individual, couple, or organization with an unclear financial situation and limited resources. The case study assignment is completed by students applying knowledge learned from the course to the specific context, and creatively applying principles to solve a financial problem.

Program 3: Continuing Education Vegetable Gardening Course

- **Service learning and project-based learning.** This course could combine service learning and project-based learning by developing a community garden in a neighborhood that does not have one but would like one. This style of project requires substantial groundwork on the part of the instructor or program ahead of time. Students in the course are responsible for developing the community garden from a reasonable beginning point. They may teach clinics for and mentor community members.
- **Problem-based learning.** This course could incorporate a series of "problems" by selecting five vegetables and then developing a set of

experiments that seek to clarify which environmental conditions optimize plant health and yield: sunlight level, starting soil nitrogen content, soil moisture, temperature, and fertilization schedule. Each week the students spend time managing their experiment plants and noting differences in their success.

- **Cooperative learning.** This course could delegate significant projects to individual students, such as "vegetable gardening at altitude" or "cold frame gardening topics." Each student could serve as an expert on his or her selected topic and develop a poster for class presentation. The poster presentations take place at a potluck where students share dishes and recipes involving vegetables they grew during the course.

These program examples intentionally leverage experiential learning techniques for transfer. Specifically, these examples prioritize engaging students in deep, active learning activities; providing time for reflection; allowing for instructor feedback and role modeling; including a highlight or culminating event; and using real-world, contextualized problems to simulate, establish, or enhance relevancy. By incorporating experiential learning techniques that align with the literature on transfer into their lessons—while also attending to individual and contextual differences in populations and classes—educators can maximize the potential for transfer.

Conclusion

Experiential learning techniques are important tools to foster transfer for adult students, but caveats remain. Learning transfer is a notoriously difficult variable for programs and instructors to influence. Packer (2001) notes that "transfer has proven hard to define, difficult to investigate, and perplexingly controversial" (p. 493). Similarly, Barnett and Ceci (2002) contend, "There is little agreement in the scholarly community about the nature of transfer, the extent to which it occurs, and the nature of its underlying mechanisms" (p. 612). Nonetheless, if deeper and more conceptual learning forms the foundation of transferable learning, then experiential learning techniques are well situated to increase transfer.

Although this chapter advocates for experiential learning techniques, we recognize that these techniques may often be less efficient instructional tools. Experiential learning is often time consuming, challenging, and inconvenient for teachers to employ; other methods of teaching (expository approaches, for instance) may be more efficient and effective for certain outcomes. In addition, some educators who do not readily identify with the "experiential" label use some of the techniques described in this chapter. These techniques are often considered good practice and are not unique to experiential learning.

Despite these caveats, experiential learning techniques provide an authentic platform for rich educational experiences that optimize the potential for transfer. Experiential learning is especially well suited to complex, divergent content and process-oriented educational outcomes. It also fits well with the needs of adult learners, who have the life experience necessary to make critical mental connections, the will to direct their own learning, and the desire to fit the educational content into an immediately relevant context. While no educator can make a student retain and apply intended lessons, by leveraging some of the inherent strengths of experiential learning techniques, educators can afford experiences that are well suited to allow adults opportunities to transfer some of the intended lessons to other times, places, and contexts in their lives.

References

Alexander, P. A., & Murphy, P. K. (1999). Nurturing the seeds of transfer: A domain specific perspective. *International Journal of Educational Research, 31*(7), 561–576.

Barnett, S. M., & Ceci, S. J. (2002). When and where do we apply what we learn? A taxonomy for far transfer. *Psychological Bulletin, 128*(4), 612–637.

Bonk, C., & Cunningham, D. J. (1998). Searching for constructivist, learner-centered and sociocultural components for collaborative educational learning tools. In C. Bonk & K. King (Eds.), *Electronic collaborators: Learner-centered technologies for literacy, apprenticeship, and discourse* (pp. 25–50). New York, NY: Erlbaum.

Boyd, E. M., & Fales, A. M. (1983). Reflective learning: Key to learning from experience. *Journal of Humanistic Psychology, 23*(2), 99–117.

Bringle, R. G., & Hatcher, J. A. (1996). Implementing service learning in higher education. *Journal of Higher Education, 67,* 221–239.

Cox, B. (1997). The rediscovery of the active learner in adaptive contexts: A developmental-historical analysis of transfer of training. *Educational Psychologist, 32*(1), 41–55.

Cranton, P. (2002). Teaching for transformation. In J. M. Ross-Gordon (Ed.), *New Directions for Adult and Continuing Education: No. 93. Contemporary viewpoints on teaching adults effectively* (pp. 63–71). San Francisco, CA: Jossey-Bass.

Fenwick, T. J. (2000). Expanding conceptions of experiential learning: A review of five contemporary perspectives on cognition. *Adult Education Quarterly, 50,* 243–272.

Frontczak, N. T. (1998). A paradigm for the selection, use, and development of experiential learning activities in marketing education. *Marketing Education Review, 8*(3), 25–33.

Haas, C., & Furman, N. (2008). Operation recreation, adventure challenge: Teaching programming through problem-based learning theory. *Schole: A Journal of Leisure Studies and Recreation Education, 23,* 60–65.

Hamm, M., & Adams, D. (1992). *The collaborative dimensions of learning.* Norwood, NJ: Ablex.

Haskell, E. H. (2001). *Transfer of learning: Cognition, instruction, and reasoning.* New York, NY: Academic Press.

Jordi, R. (2010). Reframing the concept of reflection: Consciousness, experiential learning, and reflection. *Adult Education Quarterly, 61*(2), 181–197.

Lee, C. D., & Kahnweiler, W. M. (2000). The effect of a master learning technique on the performance of transfer. *Performance Improvement Quarterly, 13*(3), 125–139.

Marienau, C., & Reed, S. C. (2008). Educator as designer: Balancing multiple teaching perspectives in the design of community based learning for adults. In S. C. Reed & C. Marienau (Eds.), *New Directions for Adult and Continuing Education: No. 118. Linking adults with community: Promoting civic engagement through community-based learning* (pp. 61–74). San Francisco, CA: Jossey-Bass.

Mayer, R., & Wittrock, M. (1996). Problem-solving transfer. In R. Calfee & D. Berliner (Eds.), *Handbook of educational psychology* (pp. 47–62). New York, NY: MacMillan.

McKeough, A., Lupart, J., & Marini, A. (1995). *Teaching for transfer: Fostering generalization in learning*. Mahwah, NJ: Erlbaum.

Packer, M. (2001). The problem of transfer, and the sociocultural critique of schooling. *Journal of Learning Sciences, 10*(4), 493–514.

Roberts, J. (2011). *Beyond learning by doing: Theoretical currents in experiential education*. New York, NY: Routledge.

Sibthorp, J., Furman, N., Paisley, K., Gookin, J., & Schumann, S. (2011). Mechanisms of learning transfer in adventure education: Qualitative results from the NOLS transfer survey. *Journal of Experiential Education, 34*(2), 109–118.

Smith, M. C. (2008). Does service learning promote adult development? Theoretical perspectives and directions for research. In S. C. Reed & C. Marienau (Eds.), *New Directions for Adult and Continuing Education: No. 118. Linking adults with community: Promoting civic engagement through community-based learning* (pp. 5–15). San Francisco, CA: Jossey-Bass.

Thomas, J. W. (2000). *A review of research on project-based learning*. San Rafael, CA: Autodesk Foundation.

NATE FURMAN *is an assistant professor and program director of the adventure education program at Green Mountain College in Poultney, Vermont.*

JIM SIBTHORP *in an associate professor in the Department of Parks, Recreation, and Tourism at the University of Utah in Salt Lake City, Utah.*

New Directions for Adult and Continuing Education • DOI: 10.1002/ace

3

This chapter provides a conceptual foundation and rationale, as well as instructional design guidelines, for using problem-based learning (PBL) to enhance adult learners' learning transfer.

Problem-Based Learning: A Learning Environment for Enhancing Learning Transfer

Woei Hung

Knowledge application and transfer is one of the ultimate instructional goals in all education settings. This goal is especially critical in adult education. Unlike K–12 students, the need for applying and transferring knowledge for college students, professional students, or workplace trainees is imminent. However, despite the effort that has been devoted to help enhance such adult learner abilities, the learning outcomes seem to remain unsatisfactory. The call for instructional interventions or strategies for alleviating students' failure to apply and transfer knowledge has never subsided (Marini & Genereux, 1995), while the demand from workplaces requiring their employees to be critical thinkers, independent problem solvers, and lifelong learners to stay competitive is on the rise. To address this issue, we will first need to understand what cognitive processes occur in a successful learning transfer and what could interfere with the processes and cause a failure of the cognitive transition.

Learning Transfer

Learning transfer is a long researched educational psychology topic since Thorndike proposed his identical elements theory in early 1900 (Schunk, 2004; Singley & Anderson, 1989). A broad definition of learning transfer may be described as applying previously learned knowledge with various degrees of adaptation or modification of that knowledge in completing a task or solving problems. Depending on the degree of the need for adaption or modification,

NEW DIRECTIONS FOR ADULT AND CONTINUING EDUCATION, no. 137, Spring 2013 © 2013 Wiley Periodicals, Inc.
Published online in Wiley Online Library (wileyonlinelibrary.com) • DOI: 10.1002/ace.20042

learning transfer can be further divided into three levels, which include knowledge application, knowledge near transfer, and knowledge far transfer. Knowledge application and transfer itself involves complex cognitive processes (Schunk, 2004). Though the process of learners' acquisition, application, and transfer of knowledge appears to be sequential and occurs naturally, the transformation from inert knowledge (Whitehead, 1929) to applicable and transferable knowledge requires a series of complex cognitive processing as well as additional supporting knowledge such as situational knowledge (Hung, 2006), strategic knowledge, and other higher order cognitive skills. Thus, educators should not assume that students' development of knowledge application and transfer ability will occur naturally. Appropriate scaffolding that provides instructional and cognitive support (e.g., an EMT instructor explicitly models diagnostic reasoning process) and fades out gradually is necessary for enhancing students' development of such abilities.

Researchers have discussed different types of learning transfer from various perspectives, such as degrees of overlapping between original and transfer contexts (near or far transfer), magnitude of knowledge being transformed (literal or figural transfer; e.g. Royer, 1979), explicit consciousness involved (low- or high-road transfer; Salomon & Perkins, 1989), or the directions of conceptualizing the learning transfer (forward- or backward-reaching transfer; e.g. Salomon & Perkins, 1989). In this chapter, I will focus on near and far transfer, as it is most commonly discussed in education fields and also most pertaining to the theme of the issue.

Near and Far Transfer. As Bassok and Holyoak (1993) argued, similarity and pragmatic relevance are two critical elements in the occurrence of transfer. Near transfer refers to a direct application of previously learned knowledge in a way that is identical or highly similar to how the knowledge was originally learned (Schunk, 2004). More specifically, near transfer involves low degrees of changes in the format and structure of tasks, complexity, or context (pragmatic application). Though near transfer is a direct application of knowledge, it involves a higher level of cognitive processing than simple recall of knowledge. In Bloom's taxonomy (Bloom, 1956), it is the application level of learning, rather than the knowledge or comprehension level of learning. The learning tasks and the corresponding performance tasks between these two levels of learning are similar but not identical. Near transfer requires a cognitive process of identifying basic elements and structure of the target problem or task, recognizing the salient similarities with previously learned knowledge, determining the most similar or applicable knowledge (Gick & Holyoak, 1987), and then executing the application. The degree of similarity and the pragmatic relevance between the original knowledge and the near transfer knowledge is high. Also, the number of variables involved in the transfer between the learning condition and performance condition is fairly low.

On the other hand, far transfer presents many more challenges for students. Though the cognitive processes of far transfer are similar to near transfer, the difficulty and complexity levels increase considerably. This increase in difficulty and complexity levels of the cognitive processes is mainly due to the decrease in the degree of salient similarity and pragmatic relevance between the forms of original knowledge and the target far transfer knowledge, the unfamiliarity of the target context, or a higher number of variables involved. More important, far transfer requires a higher degree of modification of the original knowledge than near transfer to adapt to the requirements or constraints of the target learning transfer condition. Thus, the further the differences between the two conditions and knowledge requirements, the more difficult the learning transfer is.

Obstacles of Learning Transfer. Research has shown that students have difficulty in transferring knowledge (e.g., Lecoutre, Clément, & Lecoutre, 2004) or even solving problems that were structurally identical to the problems previously learned (Gick & Holyoak, 1980; Reed, 1987). What causes the students' failure to perform such learning advances? There are a number of factors that could contribute to students' problem of transferring knowledge. First of all, in traditional teaching practice, knowledge is taught in abstract forms. Traditional teaching methods subscribe to the belief that teaching students the theories and principles is the most direct and efficient way for them to gain the fundamental conceptual knowledge of the topic under study (Jonassen, 1991). Therefore, in classrooms or training settings, the focus of teaching is on the explanations of the concepts, principles, or theories, followed by demonstrating a few examples of applying the concept or principle to solve textbook types of problems (i.e., problems in ideal conditions and with one single answer). The focus of learning is to memorize the definitions of the concept and theories, as well as comprehend them. However, application of knowledge requires more than just acquisition and comprehension of the knowledge. There is another set of knowledge and ability required for the students to transform abstract knowledge into practical application and transfer of the knowledge, which may not occur naturally for many students.

The issue of teaching and learning knowledge in abstract forms may well lead to the second possible cause to students' failure to apply and transfer knowledge. When the focus of teaching and learning is on the abstract theoretical concepts and principles, how the knowledge manifests itself in real life or how it is used to solve real-life problems may be overlooked. As a result, the traditional teaching practice often takes place in decontextualized learning environments. Without an understanding of when, where, and how the knowledge is applied, which is called situational knowledge (Hung, 2006), students are likely to experience difficulty in effectively applying the knowledge learned, let alone transfer. Thus, situational knowledge in fact accounts for the knowledge that bridges between the theoretical understanding and the practical application of the knowledge. Unfortunately, teaching and learning of situational knowledge is often absent in classrooms.

Another issue is that the problems used in traditional instruction for practice were well structured in nature. Jonassen (1997) has discussed the differences between well-structured and ill-structured problems and their instructional affordance. The basic distinctions between these two types of problems are that ill-structured problems are messy, complex, and dynamic, and possess multiple ways of interpretations and solutions, while well-structured problems are simple and linear and have one single standard answer, such as end-of-chapter problems. Solving ill-structured problems requires a certain degree of modifications of theoretical concepts or entails combinations of multiple concepts or principles. Therefore, the degree of salient similarity between the knowledge and its target application tends to be low, and pragmatic relevance is not obvious. The majority of the problems that professionals deal with in workplaces are ill structured in nature. Solving well-structured problems can help students acquire basic concepts and procedural knowledge, but it is not sufficient for enhancing their knowledge application and transfer.

Finally, the problem may lie in the instructor's and students' habit of mind. From a cognitivist point of view, the effectiveness of students' learning largely relies on an ample amount of support and scaffolding from the instructor or direct instruction. Though the theory is sound, it does not provide learning opportunities that require students (or future problem solvers) to modify, restructure, or seek further knowledge to solve the problem. Thus, the traditional fully supported instruction that is advocated by some researchers (e.g., Kirschner, Sweller, and Clark, 2006) may be effective for supporting near transfer. It, however, will fall short for far transfer learning. In a fully supported learning environment, students are likely to form a cognitive and psychological dependency on the instructor. This dependency is likely to result in a study habit of expecting fully supported direct instruction, which only requires them to acquire the readily organized knowledge set and perform direct application of it (near transfer). This study habit could weaken their development of independent, self-directed learning skills and mind-set, which are the base for the ability to spontaneously modify, restructure, or incorporate additional knowledge in responding to a novel problem.

Students' failure to transfer knowledge could be partially or fully attributed to various combinations of the issues discussed here. Problem-based learning (PBL), a constructivist yet instructionally rigorous pedagogy, may provide instructional promises to address these issues. In this chapter, I will first discuss some basic concepts of learning transfer, followed by a brief discussion of the nature and features of PBL. I will then analyze how the features of PBL could address the issues of failure of learning transfer. Finally, I will provide some instructional design guidelines for using PBL to enhance students' learning transfer.

Problem-Based Learning

Originally conceived in response to medical students' unsatisfactory clinical performances and the emphasis on memorization of fragmented knowledge in traditional medical education (Barrows & Tamblyn, 1980), PBL is an instructional method aimed at preparing students for real-world settings. With requiring students to solve problems as the main format of instruction, PBL enhances students' learning outcomes by promoting their abilities and skills in applying knowledge, solving problems, practicing higher order thinking, and self-directing and reflecting their own learning (Barrows, 1986; Hmelo-Silver, 2004; Norman & Schmidt, 1992). With the success of implementation in medical education, PBL has also been widely adopted by various disciplines in higher education as well as K–12 education settings (Hung, Jonassen, & Liu, 2008).

The Characteristics of PBL. There are five main characteristics significant for problem-based learning.

- **Problem-driven instruction.** The students' learning is initiated by the need to solve a problem. The PBL process simulates the process of solving problems. Therefore, the learning processes are embedded in the problem-solving process. This design is for the students to (a) acquire content knowledge along the way of solving the problem; (b) develop their problem-solving skills; and (c) construct their situational knowledge about when and how the content is applied in solving problems.
- **Authentic, complex, ill-structured problems.** All PBL problems are real-life complex problems, rather than well-structured, end-of-chapter-type problems. With the complexity and messiness of ill-structured problems, the students learn how to deal with the uncertainty, high degree of unknown, and no one-standard-answer nature inherent in real-life problems.
- **Problem- or case-structured curriculum.** In PBL, the content knowledge and skills to be learned are organized around problems, rather than as a hierarchical list of topics. This curriculum design helps students organize their knowledge in a case-based structure. The knowledge about the problem, symptoms, variables and concepts involved, causes, conditions, mechanism, and solutions is organized and stored in students' knowledge base as a complete problem case. This knowledge organization will not only be retrieved effectively later, but can also serve as source knowledge schemas for learning new cases or knowledge.
- **Self-directed learning.** In PBL, learning is initiated and directed mainly by the students, rather than the instructor. Students individually and collaboratively assume responsibility for generating learning objectives and processes through self-regulating their own learning processes, self-assessment, and peer assessment, and accessing their own learning materials. Also, instructors are facilitators, not knowledge disseminators.

Rather, they support and model reasoning processes, facilitate group processes and interpersonal dynamics, probe students' knowledge deeply, and do not interject content or provide direct answers to questions.

- **Reflective learning.** Reflection is a critical component in PBL. Students monitor their understanding and learn to adjust strategies for effective learning and problem solving. By engaging in metacognitive processes, the students learn how to improve their own learning. Furthermore, the reflective processes help students refine their knowledge base by summarizing the commonalities and differences between and among the problems or cases, organizing common themes among the concepts, and interconnecting related concepts and information across different problems or cases to form a complete knowledge domain (Hung, 2006; Hung, Jonassen, & Liu, 2008; Jonassen & Hung, 2012).

In summary, PBL provides learning environments where learning is problem initiated and the instruction is problem driven, and the curriculum is problem or case organized. PBL uses only authentic, complex, ill-structured problems to help students make connections between theory and real-world application, as well as develop their ability to handle the complexity of real-world problems. Students work in small groups and self-direct their own learning with instructor's guidance to practice their independent problem-solving skills. Finally, PBL emphasizes reflective learning, which is designed to cultivate students' skills and the habit of mind for lifelong learning. Now the next question is: How can PBL facilitate students to develop their ability of learning transfer? In the following, I will discuss the theoretical connections between the characteristics of PBL and the cognitive components of learning transfer, as well as how PBL can address the obstacles of learning transfer.

PBL for Facilitating Learning Transfer. The first and immediate effect is that PBL's problem-driven instruction provides a learning environment where knowledge acquisition, immediate application (near transfer), and potential novel application (far transfer) occur simultaneously. By completing a PBL process (which is a problem-solving process), the students have to immediately apply the knowledge acquired to solve the problem. Thus, in PBL, the processes of knowledge acquisition and application (near transfer) go hand-in-hand, rather than occur in separate stages. This way, the knowledge that students gain is not just theoretical concepts and principles but a set of usable working knowledge. This instructional method could reduce the students' difficulty in transferring theoretical principles into practical knowledge commonly seen in traditional classrooms.

Second, the problems to be solved in PBL are real-life, authentic problems. The main functions of this feature are to (a) contextualize the content knowledge to be learned and (b) help students establish their situational knowledge (Hung, 2006). Failure to use theoretical knowledge learned in solving a practical problem or recognize the situation where the knowledge can be applied, which is pragmatic relevance (Bassok & Holyoak, 1993), is a common problem in near learning transfer. In PBL, learning content knowledge from solving related real-life problems enables students to see how the theoretical principles are manifested in real-world settings, as well as how these principles are used in solving real-life or profession-specific problems. Therefore, contextualizing content knowledge is a process of attaching general and profession-specific meanings to the abstract theoretical principles or knowledge so that the knowledge gained is practical, rather than inert (Whitehead, 1929). With practical knowledge, the learners know what the content knowledge is for, how it looks in real-life problems, how it is used to solve problems, and, more important, when and where to apply it.

Third, PBL structured its curriculum in a problem- or case-organized manner. This curriculum design helps structure students' knowledge base as a set of related schemas that store the information about the problem cases on which they have worked. This knowledge base will consist of the related theoretical and factual knowledge, contextual information, situational knowledge, problem solving and reasoning process knowledge, solutions, and, most important, how all this knowledge and information is interconnected as a problem case. This way, the students' knowledge base is organized as a problem case library. With well-indexed situational knowledge, the student can effectively and efficiently retrieve target knowledge from his or her problem case library, which is the goal of near transfer.

Moreover, self-directed learning is a distinct feature of PBL. This feature functions to help develop students' ability of far transfer. The previous three PBL features are to help students establish an effective problem case-based knowledge, which could fulfill the demands of near transfer. However, if the situation encountered is substantially different than all the problem cases stored in the student's knowledge base, which requires far transfer, a well-established problem case library alone may be inadequate. Near transfer may only entail nonanalytic, scheme-inductive reasoning (Stolper et al., 2011), in which a well-established problem case library is essential. However, far transfer will require additional reasoning skill, which is analytic hypothetical-deductive reasoning (Stolper et al., 2011) for identifying what existing knowledge could be potentially useful and how to modify the knowledge to respond to the problem encountered. Therefore, the ability to self-direct reasoning and research will be the key in far transfer. By requiring students to conduct self-directed problem solving and learning processes, PBL helps students not only develop these self-directed learning skills but also acculturate such habits of mind.Finally, reflection is a crucial component in PBL. By incorporating this component as a routine step in the PBL process, students are engaging in the process of refining their learning results and knowledge base (schemas). This reflection process includes reflecting on their own problem-solving process, self-directed learning process, and knowledge learned. The reflection process not only helps students engage in metacognitive activities that could improve their future learning effectiveness and efficiency, but also helps the students engage in interconnecting and therefore integrating all the problem cases into a more effective knowledge schema and, more important, summarizing and conceptualizing the practical problem cases knowledge into their own implicit conceptual knowledge about the subject under study. This conceptual knowledge serves as the base for far transfer of the learning in the future.

Instructional Design Guidelines. PBL has been implemented in professional education and higher education, as well as K–12 settings. PBL is especially effective for adult learners in both traditional (e.g., college students or professional school students) and nontraditional age contexts (e.g., continuing education, working adults pursuing higher education degrees, or continuing on-the-job trainings) because the subject areas in adult learning are context specific. With the learning transfer context being specific, educators or instructional designers are able to design PBL problems with a higher degree of precision in providing students with a more effective learning experience and, in turn, enhance learning outcomes.

Though the basic principles of PBL should be applied across all levels, Hung (2011) argued that the degrees of emphasis on these principles should be calibrated to adapt to the nature of the discipline, the purpose of the learning, and the learners' cognitive readiness to optimize the learning effectiveness. Next, I offer some guidelines for using PBL to enhance adult learners' knowledge application and transfer.

Use Authentic, Contextually Meaningful Problems. All PBL problems should be real-life problems (Evenson & Hmelo-Silver, 2000; Gallagher, 1997; Gijbels, Dochy, van den Bossche, & Segers, 2005). However, this does not mean any real-life problem that could afford the intended content knowledge and learning objectives would be equally effective for adult students' knowledge application and transfer. For example, for college engineering students to study the physics concept of collision, a problem of design packaging for protecting sensitive measuring instruments for a manufacturer and a problem of designing packaging for protecting an egg to be dropped from a two-story building may seem to be equally capable of affording the concept to be learned. However, the former problem provides a direct and immediate context for the engineering students, while the latter problem is situated in a relatively remote context. As opposed to solving the former problem, the students who study by solving the latter problem will have to make an additional cross-context transition to apply the knowledge in solving the problems in their future context (or workplaces). Having students solve contextually meaningful problems would not only require them to apply the content knowledge, but also reduce unnecessary cross-context transitions for learning transfer.

Embed Profession Specifics and Culture in the Problems. When the students' future profession is apparent, the problems used should be as authentic and profession-specific as possible. This is because every profession has its own contextual specification, ways of reasoning, and primary concerns, as well as culture (Hung, 2006, 2009). For example, in a flat-screen manufacture company, the engineers in the design department and manufacturing department will have different primary concerns about a given product. Thus, besides the general contextual information that needs to be provided, the authenticity and contextual validity (Hays & Gupta, 2003) of a PBL problem should include information that will guide the students toward considering their profession-specific concern, constraints, and culture. This context component in a PBL problem (Hung, 2006, 2009) could help students see how the concepts are used in their specific profession and what possible constraints in applying them may be encountered. More important, this could help them understand how these concepts are used in different contexts (e.g., design, manufacturing, or troubleshooting), which is critical training for learning transfer.

Organize Curriculum From Immediately Applicable Contexts Gradually Outward to Remotely Applicable Contexts. As discussed earlier, application and transfer of knowledge does not come naturally or easily for most students. Especially for far transfer, the further the transfer, the more difficult it is. PBL curriculum is organized as a series of problems that cover the curriculum content, objectives, and standards. For facilitating students to develop their ability to apply and transfer knowledge learned, the curriculum should start from situating the PBL problems in the contexts where the concepts are normally applied for that discipline (or profession), and then gradually moving outward to the contexts where far learning transfer is required for solving the problem. This curriculum design is to provide appropriate scaffolding for students to gradually develop the ability of recognizing the applicability of the concepts by introducing them to immediately applicable contexts, then to near transfer contexts, and then to far transfer contexts, as well as the skills to modify the applicable concepts to respond to the problem.

Advance Higher Degree of Self-Directed Learning. One of the distinct features in PBL is self-directed learning. However, the degree of self-directedness should be learner-readiness dependent (Barrows, 1986; Hung, 2011). For adult learners, the degree of self-directed learning should be high. This is not only because the students are adults and most likely cognitively ready for self-directing in their own learning, but, more important, because the situations that require learning transfer are usually beyond school or training settings. Adult learners will soon be or are facing challenges of having to solve problems independently as well as determine what knowledge is most likely applicable and how to transfer it to a novel situation. Therefore, adult learners need to focus on developing their self-directed learning skills in order to independently self-direct their learning transfer in workplaces.

Promote Ability to Ask Effective Questions During the PBL Process. Though PBL emphasizes self-directed learning, it does not mean the instructor is not involved in the students' learning. Instead, the role of the instructor is critical in ensuring the students engage in necessary cognitive activities to achieve their learning goals. In PBL, the instructor normally guides students' problem-solving and reasoning process by prompting them with questions. In responding to the instructor's questions, the students develop their reasoning skills by modeling the instructor's reasoning patterns. However, to cultivate students' ability to independently apply and transfer knowledge, the PBL instructor should also guide them to develop such reasoning skills. One of the keys to this skill is the ability to ask effective questions. Thus, in addition to asking questions that guide the students to study intended content knowledge or to a more scientifically sound reasoning path, the instructor should also encourage them to ask themselves questions that direct their own problem-solving and reasoning process. The cognitive process of this thinking process training is similar to the cognitive process of identifying, applying, modifying, or transferring applicable knowledge to respond to a novel situation. Therefore, it is important to help students develop this skill.

Encourage Metacognition With Reflective Activities. Reflection is an important component in PBL. It is to help students improve their learning by reflecting on their problem-solving process as well as learning process. Reflection is also critical in enhancing students' learning transfer outcomes. This is because sometimes learning transfer may not happen during the formal learning process due to a number of reasons, such as distractions or cognitive overload (Sweller, 1988). Given a chance to reflect, learning transfer may come easier for some students who need more time to process what they have learned. Therefore, during the reflection phase of a PBL process, the instructor should encourage students to reflect on what they wanted to further study or try but did not have the time or the chance to do so. Mindful reflection could increase the chance for learning transfer to occur.

Conclusion

Knowledge application and transfer is one of the ultimate learning goals in education. For adult learners, these abilities are not only beneficial but also critical. The ability to apply knowledge learned from school is only a basic requirement in workplaces. In this ever-changing world, the ability to near and far transfer knowledge is the skill that keeps an individual competitive and indispensable in job markets. Therefore, in workplaces, learning transfer is not just a higher order cognitive ability; it is a survival skill. PBL is a pedagogy that could provide an effective learning environment to help students develop these skills. In this chapter, I discussed the possible causes for students' difficulty in applying and transferring knowledge, as well as how PBL could help overcome these obstacles. The instructional guidelines offered in this chapter are not an exhaustive list for addressing the issue, but, it is hoped, will serve as a starting point for further discussion and elaboration on this topic.

References

Barrows, H. S. (1986). A taxonomy of problem-based learning methods. *Medical Education, 20*, 481–486.

Barrows, H. S., & Tamblyn, R. M. (1980). *Problem-based learning: An approach to medical education.* New York, NY: Springer.

Bassok, M., & Holyoak, K. J. (1993). Pragmatic knowledge and conceptual structure: Determinants of transfer between quantitative domains. In D. K. Detterman & R. J. Sternberg (Eds.), *Transfer on trial: Intelligence, cognition, and instruction* (pp. 68–98). Norwood, NJ: Ablex.

Bloom, B. S. (1956). *Taxonomy of educational objectives handbook I: Cognitive domain.* New York, NY: McKay.

Evenson, D. H., & Hmelo-Silver, C. E. (2000). *Problem-based learning: A research perspective on learning interactions.* Mahwah, NJ: Erlbaum.

Gallagher, S. A. (1997). Problem-based learning: Where did it come from, what does it do, and where is it going? *Journal for the Education of the Gifted, 20,* 332–362.

Gick, M. L., & Holyoak, K. J. (1980). Analogical problem solving. *Cognitive Psychology, 12,* 306–355.

Gick, M. L., & Holyoak, K. J. (1987). The cognitive basis of knowledge transfer. In S. M. Cormier & J. D. Hagman (Eds.), *Transfer of learning: Contemporary research and applications* (pp. 9–46). New York, NY: Academic Press.

Gijbels, D., Dochy, F., van den Bossche, P., & Segers, M. (2005). Effects of problem-based learning: A meta-analysis from the angle of assessment. *Review of Educational Research,* 75(1), 27–61.

Hays, R., & Gupta, T. S. (2003). Ruralising medical curricula: The importance of context in problem design. *Australia Journal of Rural Health, 11,* 15–17.

Hmelo-Silver, C. E. (2004). Problem-based learning: What and how do students learn? *Educational Psychology Review,* 16(3), 235–266.

Hung, W. (2006). The 3C3R model: A conceptual framework for designing problems in PBL. *Interdisciplinary Journal of Problem-based Learning,* 1(1), 55–77.

Hung, W. (2009). The 9-step process for designing PBL problems: Application of the 3C3R model. *Educational Research Review,* 4(2), 118–141.

Hung, W. (2011). Theory to reality: A few issues in implementing problem-based learning. *Educational Technology Research & Development,* 59(4), 529–552.

Hung, W., Jonassen, D. H., & Liu, R. (2008). Problem-based learning. In M. Spector, D. Merrill, J. van Merrienböer, & M. Driscoll (Eds.), *Handbook of research on educational communications and technology* (3rd ed.; pp. 485–506). New York, NY: Erlbaum.

Jonassen, D. H. (1991). Objectivism versus constructivism: Do we need a new philosophical paradigm. *Educational Technology Research & Development,* 39(3), 5–14.

Jonassen, D. H. (1997). Instructional design models for well-structured and ill-structured problem-solving learning outcomes. *Educational Technology Research & Development,* 45(1), 65–94.

Jonassen, D. H., & Hung, W. (2012). Problem-based learning. In N. Seel (Ed.), *Encyclopedia of the sciences of learning* (pp. 2687–2690). New York, NY: Springer-Verlag.

Kirschner, P. A., Sweller, J., & Clark, R. E. (2006). Why minimal guidance during instruction does not work: An analysis of the failure of constructivist, discovery, problem-based, experiential, and inquiry-based teaching. *Educational Psychologist,* 41(2), 75–86.

Lecoutre, M.-P., Clément, E., & Lecoutre, B. (2004). Failure to construct and transfer correct representations across probability problems. *Psychological Reports,* 94(1), 151–162.

Marini, A., & Genereux, R. (1995). The challenge of teaching for transfer. In A. McKeough, J. Lupart, & A. Marini (Eds.), *Teaching for transfer: Fostering generalization in learning* (pp. 1–19). Mahwah, NJ: Erlbaum.

Norman, G. R., & Schmidt, H. G. (1992). The psychological basis of problem-based learning: A review of the evidence. *Academic Medicine,* 67(9), 557–565.

Reed, S. K. (1987). A structure mapping model for word problems. *Journal of Experimental Psychology: Learning, Memory, and Cognition, 13,* 124–139.

Royer, J. M. (1979). Theories of the transfer of learning. *Educational Psychologist, 14,* 53–69.

Salomon, G., & Perkins, D. N. (1989). Rocky road to transfer: Rethinking mechanisms of a neglected phenomenon. *Educational Psychologist, 24,* 113–142.

Schunk, D. H. (2004). *Learning theories: An educational perspective* (4th ed.). Upper Saddle River, NJ: Merrill Prentice Hall.
Singley, M. K., & Anderson, J. R. (1989). *The transfer of cognitive skills*. Cambridge, MA: Harvard University Press.
Stolper, E., Van de Wiel, M., Van Royen, P., Van Bokhoven, M., Van der Weijden, T., & Dinant, G. J. (2011). Gut feelings as a third track in general practitioners' diagnostic reasoning. *Journal of General Internal Medicine, 26*(2), 197–203.
Sweller, J. (1988). Cognitive load during problem solving: Effects on learning. *Cognitive Science, 12*, 257–285.
Whitehead, A. N. (1929). *The aims of education*. New York, NY: MacMillan.

WOEI HUNG is currently an associate professor in the Instructional Design and Technology Program at the University of North Dakota. His research areas include problem-based learning, problem solving, concept mapping and formation, and systems thinking and modeling.

4

This chapter unpacks the concept of authenticity, then discusses and illustrates how considering various elements of authenticity can help designers and trainers make more effective decisions to support learning and development.

Considering Components, Types, and Degrees of Authenticity in Designing Technology to Support Transfer

Patricia L. Hardré

We use all types of technology on a daily basis, for planning, training, and representing the concepts, procedures, and strategies in our minds to learners and others. Due to a host of factors, much of our training and instruction is being translated to digital systems and formats for delivery and implementation, or at the very least supplemented and enhanced by digital features. Authenticity is a key to using technology for instruction in ways that enhance learning and support learning transfer.

Simply put, a representation is authentic when it shows learners clearly what a task, context, or experience will be like in real practice. More authentic representations help people learn and understand better. They support learning transfer by giving learners an opportunity to see key features and reference points that show when and how tasks need to be done, and how information is relevant to actual task performance.

However, designers may need to adjust components of authenticity to optimize initial learning and eventual transfer, depending on the task, learners, and context. The following sections unpack the complex concept of authenticity, and identify some of its key components, presenting principles and strategies that inform training and learning environment design.

Authenticity is a complex characteristic, with multiple types and degrees that are important for designers and instructors to understand and leverage to optimize learning and transfer. It is a term that tends to be used loosely and broadly in teaching and training. However, if we consider authenticity closely and examine how it functions within learning environments specifically, it

NEW DIRECTIONS FOR ADULT AND CONTINUING EDUCATION, no. 137, Spring 2013 © 2013 Wiley Periodicals, Inc.
Published online in Wiley Online Library (wileyonlinelibrary.com) • DOI: 10.1002/ace.20043

can inform our design to improve both effectiveness and efficiency. Other scholars have conceptualized multiple different elements of authenticity such as for assessment (Gulikers, Bastiaens, & Kirschner, 2008), for the design of learning environments (Herrington & Oliver, 2000), and in teachers (Kreber, Klampfleitner, McCune, Bayne, & Knottenbelt, 2007). All of these efforts were based on recognition of its lack of utility for practice when treated as a unitary characteristic.

Understanding authenticity can also benefit training directors and project managers as consumers of technology tools and systems. Many training and e-learning systems make claims of authenticity, but deliver only one type or a reduced degree of potential authenticity, which limits their effectiveness in supporting transfer to authentic tasks and work environments. Considering all of the types and degrees of authenticity can save time and money for instruction and training practitioners choosing systems to represent what their learners need to do.

Defining Technology

Broadly defined, technology can include any type of tool that helps us get work done. In current use, the term most often refers to digital tools and systems, and still includes a broad range of things. Across professional training and development, higher education, and continuing and distance education, technology for learning can be anything from information written on a chalkboard, whiteboard, or glass partition, to a highly detailed three-dimensional holographic projection or a richly interactive digital simulation environment. For designers and instructors taking this broad view, instructional technology includes multiple aspects of a single-event design, such as the screenshots of a technology interface embedded in a training video, the video itself, the software in which it is developed, and the computer-based or web-based interface that delivers it. All of these levels of technology matter to instructional designers and instructors, but of particular importance for influencing learners' transfer to task is the authenticity of information and content and context presentation within all of these tools and systems.

Defining Authenticity

Authenticity here refers to the degree to which the technology (tools or systems) fully represents the actual task and context for the training needs—in other words, how realistic it is. In multimedia and technology literature, this characteristic is also referred to as *fidelity* (Alessi & Trollip, 2000). Components of authenticity include accuracy, clarity, and completeness in how the technology represents and presents both static features and functions of the task and context. These three elements of authenticity are different but related, reflected in technology elements including environment, task, communication, feedback, representation, interactivity, and information. Each component of authenticity across these elements of the technology has implications for design of instruction to support transfer.

Accuracy. *Accuracy* refers to whether elements are represented without erroneous content. Technology may be accurate but limited in scope, such as embedding screenshots of interface elements into user instructions or training materials, or a physician's partial anatomical model used to explain patients' conditions to them in the office or clinic.

Clarity. *Clarity* refers to whether the representation is recognizable and easily understood. A representation can be clear, but simplified to support cueing to the key task components (so it is not always complete). Less expert learners tend to be distracted by superficial features of an interface or problem (Bereiter & Scardamalia, 1993). For this reason, tools and models are often simplified to reduce novice learners' confusion or distraction by nonessential elements.

Completeness. *Completeness* refers to the degree to which the representation is precisely like the actual experience that the learner will have in using the skills for transfer. A complete representation will include the entire system or interface in its full complexity, including potential distractors. More complex models and representations in technology are often used either for more complex tasks or for more advanced learners.

Selecting Components of Authenticity

It is possible to design to one or more of these components of authenticity and not the others. For example, in a digital animation, a relatively simple, flat (cartoon-like) representation may be accurate in that it includes all of the key task elements that learners need to know. Such representations also tend to be clear, as they are free of any extraneous and potentially distracting elements. However, simplified representations are not complete, as they lack the nuanced distractors that will test learners for potential mistakes and misconceptions. These simplified representations are appropriate for novices in a discipline or users who are completely unfamiliar with the system. Across its components, authenticity varies in degree of detail, and it can be adjusted by degrees to more effectively support learning and transfer. Transfer to authentic use is supported by exposure to the most authentic (accurate, clear, complete) representation in training, so that possible misconceptions, distractions, and errors are exposed and remediated during instruction.

The following sections apply components of authenticity to various elements that designers and trainers need to address to optimize learning and development. These include the learning environment, cueing task initiation and action, communication, peer and instructor/facilitator feedback, representation, interactivity, and information. After examining these elements individually, I reintegrate them in an applied example.

Authenticity of the Learning Environment. In addition to considering the components and degree of authenticity of the model or system itself, designers need to consider authenticity as a characteristic of the learning environment and context. Many tasks in industry and professions occur not in a quiet office surrounded by polite listeners, but in settings that are loud and stressful and include social distractors outside of the system itself. Consider, for example, the tasks of emergency room nurses, firefighters, police, military personnel, construction workers, and production line workers such as those in the auto or meat-packing industry. Transfer to those authentic contexts-of-use is supported by first teaching the skills, then progressively moving learners to practice, and testing in similar settings. It is reasonable, initially, to expose learners to the content and skills practice in a less distracting context. However, an individual may be able to carry out skills easily in a quiet classroom with others looking on politely, but not transfer that skill to a crowded street with car noises and people shouting, or in the high-stress setting of an emergency room, when performance really matters. After the knowledge and skills are familiar, to provide authenticity in the context beyond the system, designers need to replicate the authentic setting in all of its detail and with all of its distractions to the greatest possible degree.

Authentically Cueing Task Initiation. Another consideration for authenticity is including in the design of instruction all of the critical elements of task, context, and learner perceptions that enable access and cue action. Authentic representation of the critical features of a system or context includes the signals or conditions that cue the learner to initiate the task. This type of authenticity includes physical features that allow for both visual and palpable cues, ways that learners can see and feel the problem or need. This is the way that a broken pipe, loose wire, unsecured package, or torn ligament looks and feels in the training system, or the way a tornado siren sounds or warning light appears, telling the learner that there is a need to do something, and cueing recall of the appropriate action for that need.

Authentic Communication. Communication that is authentic to the performance environment may not be conducive to initial instruction. Designers and instructors need to weigh the trade-offs among communication methods and tools. Many and diverse technology tools exist to support communication for instruction, task practice, collaboration, and feedback. These include both general and task- or field-specific tools, both hardware and software.

Some key characteristics of communication technology tools are media options and timing. Richer media options (such as audio, video, text, and graphics, with sharing capabilities) can be used for real-time practice, performance feedback, and remediation with collaborative communication. For industry, some very detailed simulation environments are equipped with internal communication systems through which distributed team members or learners can communicate and collaborate in real time, supported by feedback from an expert instructor or coach.

Timing options generally are synchronous (real time) and asynchronous (individual posting, continuous access). The former supports rapid-task

New Directions for Adult and Continuing Education • DOI: 10.1002/ace

practice and interactive communication such as over dynamic strategy revision, while the latter supports metacognitive self-awareness and individual reflection. Communication tools support transfer best when they enable effectively correcting errors and allow maximum access for learners. However, it is not the nature of the tool itself, but its fit with the task and learners that must be optimal. Dynamic communication and response are most fully authentic when they match the human-to-human *and* human-to-system interactions of the task as done in the performance context. These are most effective in supporting learning when they enable performance feedback sensitive to learners' skill levels and developing needs.

Authentic and Appropriate Feedback. In addition to the cueing for task initiation or action and team communication, designers need to leverage the potentials of technology to provide feedback that communicates how learners are progressing at learning and demonstrating the requisite knowledge and skills. Many technology systems use programmed feedback, which has an advantage in efficiency and is very effective when assessments are standardized and errors are very similar. However, customized feedback is more appropriate when assessments are generative and individualized or errors are unique among learners. Though verbal or textual feedback is the most familiar strategy, performance feedback is not limited to verbal information, and designing in authentic cueing of system errors (such as activating error warning indicator sights or sounds) can be powerful in supporting authentic transfer. Standardization of assessment characteristics is within the designer's control, but unique errors may arise among diverse learners. In general, novices learning basic skills benefit from more generalizable feedback, while more advanced learners need more nuanced and specialized feedback to refine their skills. However, needs for feedback are also subject to learners' specific related background and experience, as well as the task and content. The more standardized the content and skills to be learned, the more standardized feedback can be and still effectively support transfer. The systems and methods that provide optimal feedback for learners may be much more structured and controlled than in the performance environment. In such cases, as instructors allow more independent task work and as learners develop the ability to self-monitor their progress, feedback should be adjusted accordingly. Whether it is standardized or customized, feedback should gradually move toward being authentic to the highest degree possible, to support transfer to contexts-of-use.

Authenticity of Representation. Most professional fields use some sort of representative models of structures and systems for learning. In architecture, it is the model of a building, its interior and exterior features. It can be a traditional, three-dimensional model built out of wood and displayed on a solid platform or an interactive digital tour. In engineering, it is the prototype of a product that enables an informed critique, whether the prototype is an aluminum mock-up held in the hand or a digital prototype showing cutaways of internal features and structures. In medical education, it is the model of the human anatomy used to train surgeons, whether that is an actual human cadaver, a plastic replica of a whole body or specific anatomical features, or a digital representation of features and systems.

An authentic representation makes ideas concrete so they can be examined, handled, and experienced by learners. The instructional value of authentic representation is that it gives learners an opportunity to see, feel, and realistically experience the tasks they are learning to do. As with environmental features, both tangible models and digital representations should be designed with high clarity for novices and increasing completeness for advanced learners. At all levels, accuracy should be maintained, except when a goal of instruction is for learners to identify errors or aberrations from the normal. Of course, in diagnostic tasks (whether medical or mechanical), the indicators of abnormal circumstance are themselves authentic action cues.

Authenticity of Interactivity. For procedural skills, such as learning to use new hardware and software, screenshots are a familiar representation strategy. As actual captured images of the user interface, screenshots are visually accurate. Their clarity depends on the clarity of the interface itself. Screenshots may or may not be complete, as shots can be limited to part of the screen that learners will see when doing a task. A benefit of screenshots is their portability to print or digital instruction and support materials, while a limit is their lack of functional interactivity (which is often supplemented by highlighting, annotating, or captioning).

Traditional types of models and representations tend to be static; that is, once they are created, they stay the same. They may be manipulable, movable, or interactive in some limited ways, but most are not highly interactive. Usually, learners cannot change them in ways that show successful action or error in a task, and receive feedback that demonstrates the possible consequences of that error. Some traditional models have recently been paired with digital systems, either to provide performance feedback for manual tasks or to simulate the perceptual features of tasks using digital tools such as probes, in training such as for minimally invasive medical treatments and micro-level repairs of complex mechanical systems.

Simulations (digital models that offer the advantage of highly customized interactivity) can be used to present varying options and conditions to authentically support more refined and adaptive use of skills. They are most effective to promote transfer when the skill requires responding to different situations in different ways, such as in complex or situated problem solving. Digital simulations can offer a particularly high degree of authenticity across components, and may include multiple versions in which components of authenticity vary.

Authenticity of Information. Beyond tangible models, digital animations and simulations, and static graphics such as screenshots, narrative cases are often used to represent tasks and contexts for instruction. Cases are particularly useful when the learned skill includes some type of diagnosis (problem identification) or problem solving. Role models as case examples are also commonly used in efforts at behavior change. Cases may be presented as text or verbal language, in digital media–based formats, or in video or face-to-face role-playing with actors. Like these other types of representations, cases that support knowledge and skill transfer require a balance among the components of authenticity. In the visual arts and design, cases may take the form of photo stills with digital enhancements used to amplify clarity and focus learners' attention on key features. Once key features are identified and practiced in isolation, learners are gradually exposed to them in increasingly complete authentic contexts to support transfer. Cases can be simplified to underscore the most relevant features for learners or presented as richly authentic with many realistic nuances and distractors. As with other types of representations, simpler cases are most appropriate for novices, and more complex cases with more authentic distractors and subtle nuances are more appropriate as learners develop greater expertise.

Applied Examples

To illustrate application of these elements of authenticity in technology, consider the meta-skill of public speaking or group presentation, an essential competency for professionals from business to education, from journalism to engineering, from arts to health sciences. A common use of technology for instruction in speaking and presentation is videotaping and viewing for critique (self, peer, expert, or group). Videotaping speakers and presenters provides the speaker with audience perspective, addressing the authenticity components of *accuracy* and *clarity* for the learner. However, elements of the *completeness* component of authenticity for this particular skill focus on audience and physical context or media.

Videotaping may be done in relative isolation (alone or in a room with the teacher or coach and perhaps a few peers), or in an actual classroom, conference room, or hall, with a proxy audience or with real learners or clients. The latter context (actual space, real clients) is the most complete in authenticity and can cue the most vivid nerves, insecurities, errors, and distractions for learners to work through. However, the logistics of gathering and scheduling this type of audience are often problematic. Digital presentation systems can arguably be used to reach a more authentic audience (and reduce *some* of the challenging logistics), but they add the complexity of digital interface. The authenticity of this choice depends on the probable match with the performance context. If actual presentations in the profession are still most frequently face to face, then match is poor and accuracy and completeness are low. If the tool in training is similar to those used in the profession, it has more complete instructional authenticity. For learners in business who expect to work on distributed teams and present in such systems, they may be fully authentic; whereas for classroom teachers or laboratory researchers working primarily with on-site teams, they may be less authentic. Using digital contexts that are somewhat artificial on the media side introduces trade-offs between goals such as reaching an audience and providing a fully authentic context for practice.

Even if it is a good match and very authentic, once again using digital technology with very novice presenters early on may lack clarity that supports their initial focus on foundational skills or key features. Technology can distract if introduced too early. Based on characteristics of the skill or task and the learners, it may be critical to ground them clearly in basics first, and then introduce the complexities of digital systems and very complete authentic elements such as audience.

Similarly, there are a number of software products available to specifically support nonnative language learning, used across language-learning settings. Learners can listen to pronunciation of words and phrases and they can record and listen to themselves. While the most authentic setting is live conversation, it is difficult to provide systematic, independent practice and support for each learner. Technology-based systems can provide an opportunity for frequent and independent practice and repetition, but they also add technical demands and introduce shifts in elements of authenticity. Instructors need to prepare learners to use technology for learning, including addressing these shifts. As standardized testing moves to digital formats, instructors need to not only facilitate acquisition of required knowledge and skill, but also prepare learners for the unique demands of computer-based assessment.

A similar set of issues surrounding authenticity arise in the use of various models and simulation systems for training such as in medical and surgical education. Medical product companies have rushed to create and test training tools that address a host of issues facing medical schools and physicians' continuing education. These tools range from simple, static anatomical models to those that include digital probes and error feedback systems. A high degree of their effectiveness depends on how the elements of authenticity match both the current needs of learners and the nature and context of the eventual performance task. Initially, medical students are most often *novices in the task*, though they may have experience with other probe-based interactive systems. In contrast, practicing physicians learning on the same models may be relatively expert in the diagnostic or surgical task, but *unfamiliar with the digital feedback system*. Familiarity with both elements (the basic model and the more complex context or system) is key to their design appropriateness and implementation, as is the match of both elements to learners' actual performance. Using a sophisticated digital feedback system is an important element of authenticity if the learner will use such a system on actual patients. However, the same system may actually distract novice physicians from attending to other sources of information while learning the task basics, a circumstance that could result in error when performing the procedure without that feedback system. If it is not clear what the circumstances of performance will be, one strategy is for learners to practice and test on new procedures both with and without the digital probes and feedback.

New Directions for Adult and Continuing Education • DOI: 10.1002/ace

Summary

Technology supports learning transfer when it represents key features with the right degree of the various elements of authenticity for the learner, task, and context. Accuracy, freedom from erroneous elements, is equally necessary for all learners. Clarity is critical for more novice learners, as they attend to key characteristics and are learning foundational principles and recognizing basic cues for action. Completeness is critical for more advanced learners as they develop more refined skills and move toward transfer to authentic and independent use because they need to be exposed to the full complexity of performance conditions. Too much detail too early can disrupt initial learning and cause distraction and confusion, while insufficient detail later on reduces transfer of learning through a lack of authentic understanding of the conditions and context-of-use. Considerations of authenticity need to include not only the immediate environment and content, along with task representation, but also surrounding context and systems, to fully support learners' transfer to task performance.

References

Alessi, S. M., & Trollip, S. R. (2000). *Multimedia for learning: Methods and development* (3rd ed). Needham Heights, MA: Allyn & Bacon.

Bereiter, C., & Scardamalia, M. (1993). *Surpassing ourselves: An inquiry into the nature and implications of expertise*. Chicago, IL: Open Court.

Gulikers, J., Bastiaens, T., & Kirschner, T. (2008). Defining authentic assessment: Five dimensions of authenticity. In A. Havnes & L. McDowell (Eds.), *Balancing dilemmas in assessment and learning in contemporary education* (pp. 73–86). London, England: Routledge.

Herrington, J., & Oliver, R. (2000). An instructional design framework for authentic learning environments. *Educational Technology Research and Development, 48*(3), 23–48.

Kreber, C., Klampfleitner, M., McCune, V., Bayne, S., & Knottenbelt, M. (2007). What do you mean by "authentic"? A comparative review of the literature on conceptions of authenticity. *Adult Education Quarterly, 58*(1), 22–43.

PATRICIA L. HARDRÉ *is professor of instructional psychology and technology, and associate dean of graduate programs and research, in the Jeannine Rainbolt College of Education at the University of Oklahoma.*

5

This chapter describes how we can create brain-friendly learning environments and become brain-friendly educators based on knowledge of how the human brain works.

Brain-Friendly Teaching Supports Learning Transfer

Jacqueline McGinty, Jean Radin, Karen Kaminski

The human brain is an active processor of information. When encountering new stimuli, the dendrites of the brain grow and synapses are created between neurons (Gunn, Richburg, & Smilkstein, 2007). Knowledge of how the brain works can help educators create brain-friendly learning environments that will enhance learning and the likelihood of transfer.

The Relationship Between Cognitive Theory and Learning Transfer

Based on knowledge about how the brain works, the practice of learning and applying information to new situations is a multifaceted process of making connections. Designing instruction that is compatible with the brain's natural processes includes giving attention to the fact that the brain adapts and adjusts when it encounters new information. One of the most important aspects of teaching and learning is the concept of *learning transfer*, or the application of prior learning to new and different situations. Too often, "Learners can recite rote material back in its memorized form, such as names and dates in a history course, but typically do not understand the concepts implicit in the material and cannot transfer or apply that knowledge in a thoughtful or creative way" (Gunn et al., 2007, p. 56).

Applying conceptual understanding from one setting to the next requires students to utilize the brain's capacity to build new neural networks (Figure 5.1). The building of neural networks is fostered from continual inquiry and the process of discovery.

NEW DIRECTIONS FOR ADULT AND CONTINUING EDUCATION, no. 137, Spring 2013 © 2013 Wiley Periodicals, Inc.
Published online in Wiley Online Library (wileyonlinelibrary.com) • DOI: 10.1002/ace.20044

Figure 5.1. The Difference Between a Neuron That Has Been Trained and One That Has Not.

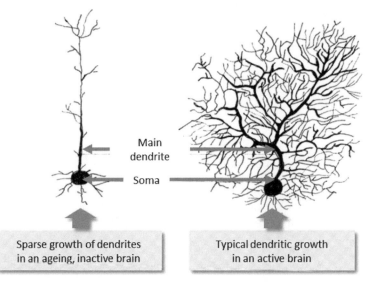

Main
dendrite

Soma

Sparse growth of dendrites
in an ageing, inactive brain

Typical dendritic growth
in an active brain

Source: A. C. Lamont and G. M. Eadie (2011). Copyright 2011 by Healthy Memory Company Ltd. Reprinted with permission.

Schema theory rests on the assumption that students utilize prior knowledge as a foundation for processing new information. The brain is a natural problem solver and, if engaged properly, will seek new and novel ways to solve complex problems. The educator can design instruction to utilize the brain's natural problem-solving tendencies by encouraging students to activate prior knowledge, make associations, connect emotionally, and foster curiosity. "If we elaborate our learning by thinking about its relationship to other things we know or by talking about it—explaining, summarizing, or questioning—we are more likely to remember it when we need to use it later" (Svinicki & McKeachie, 2011, p. 36).

How humans relate to the world has a direct relationship with learning and development. Social cognitive theory suggests that humans develop in relationship to social interaction. According to the social cognitive perspective, there is a constant interaction of personal, behavioral, and environmental factors. It is suggested that while humans can learn by asocial trial-and-error methods, successful skill development would not occur without interaction with knowledgeable others (Nielsen, Subaiul, Galef, Zentall, & Whiten, 2012). In addition to social influences on thought and behavior is the cognitive aspect of social cognitive theory in which:

> . . . cognitive factors partly determine which environmental events will be observed, what meaning will be conferred on them, whether they will leave lasting effects, what emotions impact and motivating power they have, and how

the information they convey will be organized for future use. (Bandura, 2009, p. 95)

For educators, the key to creating an enriched environment for learning is to understand how the brain functions and learns, and then to put those understandings to practical use. In this chapter, we provide guidance on creating brain-friendly learning environments and identify characteristics of brain-friendly learning facilitators. In addition, we explain how cognitive learning and brain-friendly environments foster learning transfer.

Brain-Friendly Learning Environments

To promote dendritic growth (Figure 5.1), the brain requires stimulation, novelty, and problem-solving opportunities. An environment that has mostly predictable or repetitive stimuli fosters boredom in the brain, making it turn inward for new and novel stimuli (Sousa, 2011). "Recent work on brain development and learning suggests that the most effective adult educators may be unwitting neuroscientists who use their interpersonal skills to tailor enriched environments that enhance brain development" (Cozolino & Sprokay, 2006, p. 11). Creating an *enriched environment* in the classroom is vital to brain growth and hence student achievement. It consists of opportunities for students to tap into all of the senses to learn, in an environment that is nonthreatening. Above all, an enriched environment allows the learner to be an active participant rather than a passive observer (Diamond & Hopson, 1998). Brain-friendly educators naturally understand the importance of positive social interaction and shared experiences.

Creating Brain-Friendly Learning Environments. Creating a brain-friendly learning environment should be purposeful. Both tangible and intangible components support student learning and hence transfer of learning. The tangible components can consist of clean, well-lighted classrooms that are pleasant smelling, well laid out for multiple uses, and aesthetically pleasing, and that contain multiple resources for topics currently under study (Hoge, 2002; Kovalik & Olsen, 1998). Thinking about how the desks or tables are arranged can automatically set the tone for learning: A large circle invites everyone to participate; the "double doughnut" arrangement promotes partner work and dialogue; tables with four to six chairs apiece are optimal for group work and discussion. A comfortable room temperature is crucial. It is difficult, if not impossible, to be attentive in a room that is too hot or too cold. Providing good reading light, colorful posters and artwork, plants, and interesting objects related to the topic at hand all draw learners in. However, try not to overdo with too much stimulation! Save some of the posters for another session, space out guest speakers so that students have time to process their message, and remember that some students find constant change disconcerting. The tangible components are easily achieved with some reflection and preparation. The intangible components are even more important but harder to create. These include a safe, nonthreatening environment, others' interest in success, social interaction, active engagement in hands-on and minds-on learning, integration of multiple intelligences, opportunities for inquiry and problem solving, and real-life relevant activities (Cozolino & Sprokay, 2006; Given, 2002).

Learning Community. The most fundamental step toward creating an enriched environment is to spend time throughout the semester building a *learning community.* In many classrooms, particularly in postsecondary settings, this important step is often overlooked. The emphasis is usually on delivery of the content. Educators forget that they are teaching people first and content second. A good way to get students immediately interacting with each other is to have each student make a large folded name tag, seat the students in small groups of four to six the first day of class, and challenge them to discover something they all have in common (besides the obvious commonality of being students). This technique immediately gets students interacting in a nonthreatening way. You can have each group name themselves and refer to them throughout the first class session as the "music lovers," the "Wyoming group," or the "traveled farthest to be there." Have the students discuss with a partner what they perceive a learning community to be. This gets everyone on board and sets the stage for future classes and lets the students know that, as in the workplace, social collaboration, respect for others, and other values will be important in their learning. Encourage everyone to learn names as quickly as possible, which, of course, you will model. The key concept is to "go slow in order to go fast." The time spent on building a strong learning community will pay dividends throughout the learning event.

Another technique that has been successful is to have each student make a small mini-poster that depicts three interesting things about himself or herself. The three interesting things can be magazine cutouts, original drawings, or simply words. For example, the educator's mini-poster might include his or her name, a picture of a woman kayaking, the words *family* and *learning,* and a simple drawing of a dog. After presenting the mini-poster to the entire class, you can invite each student to share his or hers, with a short question-and-answer period following each presentation. After explaining that the brain can best remember a series of six to seven presentations, each mini-poster is taped to the classroom wall quilt-style, with each poster touching others. This provides a visual representation of how our developing learning community is growing and how we are all connected to each other. Students find this unusual and powerful.

Emotions. Emotions play a critical role in learning, how students feel about learning, and retention. Keeping this in mind, educators are challenged to design instruction that engages student interest and emotion. The brain resists having meaningless, noncontextual information and facts imposed on it. One way to enhance meaning and memory is to have learners share their personal experiences relating the content to real-life problems. Another way to integrate positive emotions is by incorporating rituals into the classroom routine (Roberts, 2002). These can be as simple as rating your day as a weather report (i.e., "partly cloudy," "sunny with a chance of rain," "tsunami!") and sharing the report with the class (which gives you valuable feedback about the class climate) to routines involved with lesson closure. Whatever you choose, you should model enthusiasm and passion and guide and mentor your students in supportive ways (Daloz, 1999; Smilkstein, 2001).

Fear and pleasure are the two emotions for which researchers have found specific brain sites that are in communication with one another. Emotion regulators in the brain include the brain stem, the limbic system, and the cerebral cortex (LeDoux, 1996). The brain stem, which monitors involuntary activity, keeps the brain at a general level of attention by filtering incoming sensory information. The limbic system, associated with emotion and memory processing, is linked to several other modules, including the frontal lobes in the cerebral cortex. Sylwester (1994) notes that the limbic system "is powerful enough to override both rational thought and innate brain response patterns. In short, we tend to follow our feelings" (p. 63). He also notes that the frontal lobes are important in the regulation of the body's emotional states and judgments, even to the extent that they can override undesirable and automatic behaviors. As part of an enriched environment, creating an atmosphere of acceptance, encouragement, and support is crucial. Brain-friendly learning includes mind-to-mind and heart-to-heart connections (Cozolino & Sprokay, 2006). Making the classroom an emotionally safe place to be in turn creates a desire for learning. Adrenaline enhances the memory of the experience. This works in positive as well as stressful events. Therefore, incorporating activities that lead to positive emotional experiences will create more vivid memories, and the potential for learning and transfer are increased.

Stress. Directly related to the role of emotions in learning is the role of stress and threat. Biologically, when fearful sensory input enters the brain, the autonomic system and stress hormones are activated. The thalamus relays immediate input to the amygdala, the emotional center of the brain. Depending on whether the amygdala perceives the incoming stimuli as threatening or not, signals are sent to the cortex to deal with the threat rationally, or the amygdala bypasses the cortex to deal with the threat in a "knee-jerk" reaction (Ratey, 2002). During this process, adrenaline, vasopressin, and cortisol are released throughout the body, causing changes in the way we think, feel, and act. A typical biochemical response to a perceived threat, whether physical, environmental, academic, or emotional, is the "fight, freeze, or flee" response. The key term here is the word *perceived.* What one person perceives as a threat may not threaten another person. A list of possible student threats and stressors are such issues as home life, personal relationships, harassment, racism, bullying and abuse, and health concerns. Learning-related stressors are often perceived as noncaring or nonresponsive educators, homework deadlines, peer pressure, the potential for humiliation or embarrassment, feelings of inferiority, and lack of self-efficacy. Bandura (2001) suggests that learners can become inhibited if they perceive they will not be successful at a given task. When students are expected to learn in a threatening or stressful setting, learning may be inhibited and narrowed. The results can be a state of helplessness, wherein students become less aware of their surroundings and contexts, and turn inward to protect themselves from further threat. In addition, "individuals with difficult life experiences sometimes learn to be very observant and to attribute meaning to the tone associated with statements, to the implied meaning of terms, to the signals of posture, or to other nonverbal behaviors" (Svinicki & McKeachie, 2011, p. 156). They essentially shut down.

The implication for adult educators is the fact that a caring and passionate mentor may help keep the brain positively engaged, leading to more meaningful learning. As a learning facilitator, carefully consider your wording of questions and your physical as well as verbal responses to students.

> It is becoming more evident that through emotional facial expressions, physical contact, and eye gaze—even through pupil dilation and blushing—people are in constant, if often unconscious, two-way communication with those around them. It is in the matrix of this contact that brains are sculpted, balanced, and made healthy. (Cozolino & Sprokay, 2006, p. 13)

To address the stress-threat balance, educators should strive for a state of *relaxed alertness*, which combines high challenge and low threat. This requires helping your learners gain self-awareness so they can identify and externalize these stressors. This is not an easy thing to achieve, as it is totally contextual. Only you can determine how to best do this in your educational setting. Here are a few tried-and-true ideas to help you address stress and threat issues. Emphasizing relationship building between peer-peer and educator-student (again, the safe learning community), classroom routines and rituals, and good time management go a long way in alleviating stress. Students do not appreciate surprises! A simple thing you can do to help yourself and your class is to provide an agenda. This can include a "coming-to-presence" activity, schedule for the day, reminders about future tasks or assignments, when the coffee break will occur, and other important happenings. A coming-to-presence activity at the beginning of class gives everyone a chance to relax and reconnect. This can be sharing a recent experience or story, a provocative question or quote, a funny cartoon, or anything that relates to your content and gets students emotionally involved.

Teaching Methods. Sousa's (2011) belief that "if something is worth teaching, it is worth teaching well" underscores the need to aid learning transfer through effective teaching methods. Incorporating sound or music, activities or games, drama, stories, and simulations into instruction all strengthen the intangible components of an enriched environment. Utilizing instruction that is rich in imagery helps to explain complex concepts and helps students to make associations that they would not normally make. Helping students make personal connections to their work through narratives, journals, discussions,

New Directions for Adult and Continuing Education • DOI: 10.1002/ace

sharing, and reflection is also important, as well as providing opportunities for metacognitive and self-regulatory activities (Smilkstein, 2001; Sousa, 2011). The more students learn about themselves and how they learn, the more easily they will be able to transfer these skills and learnings to other settings. Students are often amazed and sometimes relieved when they learn about how they themselves learn. These discoveries can help explain problems or successes in the past, and also transfer into the workplace where individuals interact with coworkers who may have completely different styles or strengths.

Providing a complete syllabus, rubrics, and clear explanations and expectations is greatly appreciated by most students. Facilitate learning in multiple forms, allowing for those who learn best in audio, visual, or kinesthetic forms to excel. Variety keeps the content stimulating; therefore, switch off between small groups, guest speakers, panels, individual reflection, lecture, discussion, case study, and experiential opportunities. Present assignments in many modalities: explain it, give examples, post the requirements online, and revisit the assignment a week or two before it is due to answer any questions. Adult learners have a full plate of responsibilities and will be glad that you have thoughtfully structured your class time and class work to be respectful of their busy lives.

Characteristics of Brain-Friendly Learning Facilitators. Brain-friendly learning facilitators are those who are concerned not only about the content and environment but also how they personally affect learning outcomes. Specifically, successful facilitators are well prepared and excited about the content, maintain a positive attitude, and are good listeners.

Preparation. Learning needs to be engaging for all ages of learners; it needs to be applicable and take into consideration that all students learn at a different pace and in a different way. An individual's schema represents his or her existing knowledge about concepts. This includes objects and their relationships with other objects, skills and sequences of skills, and events and sequences of events. Sometimes it will be easy for students to tie new learning to their existing schemata (an example of schema theory is presented in Chapter 1 of this issue). Other times you may find that you need to step back and help them with necessary prior learning, or even unlearning, before they are ready to learn. Students may have prior experiences that are contradictory of the new learning, strong beliefs that are contrary to what is being taught, and fears about returning to formal or informal learning based on prior experiences.

> Although adults continue to acquire new knowledge and skills, they must integrate new experience with prior learning. When this integration does not occur easily and contradictions or dilemmas result, the prior learning must be examined and some adjustments made. Individuals can reject the contradictory new information or revise their previous views. This, simply stated, is the process of reflection and transformative learning. (Cranton, 2006, p. 22)

You need to help your students understand their existing schemata and how it developed, and to find ways to tie the new learning in. This includes asking them individually of their experiences and helping them realize they can learn (it is never too late). Listen, let students tell their own story, and be cognizant of their needs. You then need to help them make meaning of their learning and apply it to their work, life, or community settings.

Transfer is much more likely to occur if the student is engaged in the learning process and understands how the new knowledge and skills can be applied. One key aspect is being well versed in the content or topic that you are teaching. The ability to present in depth and from multiple perspectives, in multiple forms, will give each student the opportunity to grasp the concept. Have many ideas on how to share the information so you can try something different when needed. Activities should be authentic and help students gain understanding in how the knowledge and skills can be applied in life or work. It is important to know the full sequence of learning and meet the students where they are in initiating their own learning process. Be prepared to cover foundational content or to skip ahead, depending on where your learners are. Plan to provide opportunities for the learners to practice using their new knowledge and skills and apply them to new settings.

Additionally, you should be well connected and informed in the community and able to share information on resources and support services outside of the scope of the content. While you build relationships with your students, also know your limits and boundaries, directing individuals to the appropriate support systems when needed.

Attitude and Listening. Maintain a positive and supportive attitude. If you are interested in the content and portray its importance, it will be easier for your participants to make the connections. Your learners will have varied backgrounds and experience. Mezirow (1991) suggests that all questions are valid questions and nothing should be taken for granted. "When a teacher presents a new concept or skill in class, students from a culture or educational background different from the teacher's might not have the requisite, preliminary, foundation knowledge upon which to construct the new knowledge" (Gunn et al., 2007, p. 68). Maintain a positive environment where understanding and meaning of experiences is acquired and validated through human interaction and communication (Mezirow, 1991). You can acknowledge that all questions are good and all perspectives are valid, and support your students in their quest for understanding.

McClusky's (1963) theory of margin reminds us how important it is to listen to our learners. His theory is simple: An individual's margin or capacity to take on additional events such as learning is the relationship between load (self and social demands) and power (the resources an individual can depend on). As educators in adult learning settings, you need to be cognizant of the load each of your students is experiencing and the support systems they have in place. Family, work, and finances can be motivators for learning while at the same time distracters. Listen to your learners and observe the unspoken messages that they provide for you. While working on creating a safe and engaging environment, remain diligent throughout the learning event, constantly monitoring students' level of comfort and attention to learning. Brain-friendly facilitators remain aware of students' physical needs in addition to their learning needs. Depending on the setting you work in, the content you are facilitating may be very flexible for students' needs, such as times they are learning for personal gain or interest. Other times, it may be driven by an organizational need. Student need and motivation may differ greatly if the student is required to be there or if the student has chosen to be there. If you can discover the motivations that brought the students to the educational experience, you can build on those initial driving forces and expand the learning in relevant and meaningful ways.

Underresourced students are those who lack necessary support structures both financially and socially and have difficulties securing other resources needed for academic success. Underresourced learners tend to have lower levels of education. They do not "preplan" their learning but use what occurs at the time needed. If your students are distracted by stress, fear, or other challenges in their life, learning and therefore potential for transfer will be disrupted. As a brain-friendly educator, you will possess strong interpersonal relationship skills. Commit to personal development in the areas of communication and empathy, facilitating from both a knowledgeable and caring perspective. Recognize that individual development is facilitated by a relationship of caring between teachers and students, and you will be able to reach *all* of your students (Daloz, 1999).

Conclusion

Developing instruction that promotes learning transfer begins by setting the stage for increased understanding and relevance. By utilizing the brain's natural learning processes, educators can integrate strategies designed to build connections. Individuals who come to the learning environment hold a variety of schemata. You should consider the background of your students to include cultural factors, current knowledge, and prior learning experiences. To create new knowledge, students need to be able to connect to what they already know. "The brain is a dynamic creation that is constantly organizing and reorganizing itself when it receives new stimuli" (Sousa, 2011, p. 143). It is the task of the brain-based educator to discover the foundational knowledge of the student and to encourage the making of the connections.

Brain-based instruction recognizes the fact that learning develops with the increase of neural networks and creates experiences where students can make connections between new and prior learning (see Figure 5.2). "Making teaching culturally responsive involves strategies such as constructing and designing relevant cultural metaphors and multicultural representations to help bridge

Figure 5.2. An Example of Using Metaphors.

When teaching human nutrition, learners may encounter difficulties with the concepts presented unless they can relate the processes to familiar experience. Many adult learners can grasp the concept of driving and owning a car but have more difficulty understanding the relationships between food and fuel for the body. Developing instruction that relates the importance of putting the right gas in your car to the importance of putting the proper food into one's body helps to build bridges between what students already know and the new concepts being learned. The concept of putting the wrong gas into a car or forgetting to change the oil in an automobile can easily be related to the outcomes that arise when one eats the wrong foods or doesn't care for the body properly.

the gap between what students already know and appreciate and what they will be taught" (Hawley & Rollie, 2007, p. 176).

In the process of creating environments that build trust, you should include activities that foster curiosity. "Curiosity sustains the mental effort that they must put forth in order to solve the problem and learn the material" (Svinicki & McKeachie, 2011, p. 190). When students are given the opportunity to empathize and make personal connections with the information being presented and can internalize the experience, the learning becomes deeper and more tangible.

Make sure to offer a variety of experiences and learning activities to allow all students the opportunity to excel. Use differentiated examples and instructional methods that will assist with creating safe learning environments and allow for introduction of diverse curriculum that will fit the needs of the students as individuals. Create active learning situations and use opening questions that allow students to relate new material to their prior experiences to aid in learning transfer. Build in the intentional practice of learning transfer, allowing for time to practice applying the new knowledge and skills to similar settings or every day events. Then practice applying them to new settings or more challenging settings. Finally, provide time for reflection on the experience to provoke transfer of learning.

New Directions for Adult and Continuing Education • DOI: 10.1002/ace

References

Bandura, A. (2001). Social cognitive theory: An agentic perspective. *Annual Review of Psychology, 52*, 1–26.

Bandura A. (2009). Social cognitive theory of mass communication. In J. Bryant & M. B. Oliver (Eds.), *Media Effects: Advances in Theory and Research* (3rd ed; pp. 94–124). New York, NY: Routledge.

Cozolino, L., & Sprokay, S. (2006). Neuroscience and adult learning. In S. Johnson & K. Taylor (Eds.), *New Directions for Adult and Continuing Education: No. 110. The neuroscience of adult learning* (pp. 11–19). San Francisco, CA: Jossey-Bass.

Cranton, P. (2006). *Understanding and promoting transformative learning: A guide for educators of adults* (2nd ed). San Francisco, CA: Jossey-Bass.

Daloz, L. A. (1999). *Mentor: Guiding the journey of adult learners* (2nd ed). San Francisco, CA: Jossey-Bass.

Diamond, M., & Hopson, J. (1998). *Magic trees of the mind.* New York, NY: Dutton.

Given, B. (2002). *Teaching to the brain's natural learning systems.* Alexandria, VA: Association for Supervision and Curriculum Development.

Gunn, A., Richburg, R., & Smilkstein, R. (2007). *Igniting student potential: Teaching with the brains natural learning processes.* Thousand Oaks, CA: Corwin Press.

Hawley, W., & Rollie, D. (2007). *The keys to effective schools: Educational reform as continuous improvement.* Thousand Oaks, CA: Corwin.

Hoge, P. (2002). The integration of brain-based learning and literacy acquisition. *Dissertation Abstracts International: Section A. Humanities and Social Sciences, 63*(11), 3069680.

Kovalik, S., & Olsen, K. (1998). How emotions run us, our students, and our classrooms. *NASSP Bulletin, 82*(598), 29–37.

Lamont, A. C., & Eadie, G. M. (2011). *Seven second memory: Memory techniques that will change your life* (3rd ed). Auckland, New Zealand: Healthy Memory Company Ltd.

LeDoux, J. (1996). *The emotional brain: The mysterious underpinnings of emotional life.* New York, NY: Simon & Schuster.

McClusky, H. Y. (1963). The course of the adult life span. In W. C. Hallenbeck (Ed.), *Psychology of adults* (pp. 10–20). Chicago, IL: Adult Education Association of the U.S.A.

Mezirow, J. (1991). *Transformative dimensions of adult learning.* San Francisco, CA: Jossey-Bass.

Nielsen, M., Subaiul, F., Galef, B., Zentall, T., & Whiten, A. (2012). Social learning in humans and nonhuman animals: Theoretical and empirical dissections. *Journal of Comparative Psychology, 126*(2), 109–113.

Ratey, J. (2002). *A user's guide to the brain.* New York, NY: Vintage Press.

Roberts, J. (2002). Beyond learning by doing: The brain compatible approach. *Journal of Experiential Education, 25*(2), 281–285.

Smilkstein, R. (2001). How the brain learns: Research, theory, and application. *Learning Assistance Review, 6*(1), 24–38.

Sousa, D. (2011). *How the brain learns.* Thousand Oaks, CA: Corwin Press.

Svinicki, M., & McKeachie, W. (2011). *McKeachie's teaching tips: Strategies, research, and theory for college and university teachers* (13th ed). Belmont, CA: Wadsworth.

Sylwester, R. (1994). How emotions affect learning. *Educational Leadership, 52*(2), 60–65.

JACQUELINE MCGINTY *is a doctoral student in the School of Education at Colorado State University.*

JEAN RADIN *is a private educational consultant and was a public school teacher and university adjunct professor for 33 years.*

KAREN KAMINSKI *is the chair of the Master of Education in Adult Education and Training in the School of Education at Colorado State University.*

6

Racial and cultural influences on learning transfer have rarely been addressed. This chapter explores theoretical, anecdotal, and the limited empirical evidence for the influence of these factors and their implications for learning transfer in adult education practice.

Racial and Cultural Factors and Learning Transfer

Rosemary Closson

Baldwin and Ford (1988) specifically include learner characteristics as one of three key inputs into the learning transfer process but infrequently (actually almost never) has race, ethnicity, or culture been included as a variable when describing trainee characteristics. For the most part we are left to speculate as to the potential influence that race, ethnicity, or cultural differences might have on the learning transfer process. Caffarella (2002) is one of the very few adult educators who address learning transfer and identify cultural difference as a factor that may influence transfer. It is time we consider this more deeply. This chapter introduces and explores thoughts on how racial or cultural dif- *purpose* ferences can potentially influence learning transfer. Keeping in mind that the field of adult education covers a wide swath of territory, we have to convert the language of learning transfer, which is crafted largely in the business and industry sector, to be more legible in the numerous other environments in which adult educators work. Typically, transfer is spoken of as training transfer within an organization. In this chapter, learning transfer is discussed within contexts such as publicly run agencies or nonprofit service-oriented organizations. Further, because adult educators work outside of the United States, often with nondominant persons, it is important to consider the international context and how lack of status, education, and wealth may influence the learning transaction and, by extension, learning transfer. The chapter closes with suggestions for adult education practitioners.

An initial reader response to the conjecture that race or culture could influence learning transfer might be that race is a social construct (almost any anthropology or sociology text confirms this) and therefore without substance. However, race, at least in the United States, has historic salience and a legal

NEW DIRECTIONS FOR ADULT AND CONTINUING EDUCATION, no. 137, Spring 2013 © 2013 Wiley Periodicals, Inc.
Published online in Wiley Online Library (wileyonlinelibrary.com) • DOI: 10.1002/ace.20045

legacy (key among which are *Brown v. Board of Education,* 1954; Title VII of the Civil Rights Act of 1964; and state-level affirmative action policies, many of which are now overturned or modified). A helpful definition of (race) is this from Haney Lopez (1994): "Race is neither an essence nor an illusion, but rather an on-going, contradictory, self-reinforcing, plastic process subject to the macro forces of social and political struggle and the micro effects of daily decisions" (p. 3). Haney Lopez's definition importantly underscores the macro influence of social forces and the micro influence of our personal choices in creating race. At the macro level, the evidence of systemic racism is tangible. One example is demonstrated in a Pew Research Center analysis illuminating a huge disparity between Black, Hispanic, and White median household net worth in 2009: White, $113,149; Hispanic, $6,325; and Black, $5,677 (Kochhar, Fry, & Taylor, 2011). Unemployment in 2010 was highest for Black Americans at 16%, Hispanics at 12.5%, and Whites at 8.7% (United States Department of Labor, 2010). Black unemployment, when compared to Whites, is almost twice as high, and median household net worth of Whites is nearly 20 times higher than that of Black households.

The three primary influences on learning transfer according to the Baldwin and Ford (1988) model are the trainee's characteristics, the training design, and the work environment. Not only are race and culture of the trainee critical considerations for influencing learning transfer, but we also need to consider that learning transfer, in part, depends on the context where the learning is to be applied. The context too can be affected by racism, and thus here lies another possible inhibitor to a learner's efforts to transfer learning.

When attempting to understand the possible effects of race, culture, or ethnicity on the learning transaction, it is helpful to review all of the elements that constitute a learning transaction because each has a part to play in how race or racism and culture can affect the learning transfer process.

The Learning Transaction

The learning transaction, regardless of where it takes place, can be described as a relationship between *teacher and his or her ideals, learner, and content,* which occurs within a *context* (Pratt, 1998). Let us briefly examine each of these elements, in relation to race and culture, to see how they might potentially influence the learning transaction.

Adult Educator's Perception of the Learning Transaction. The adult educator's perception of the learning transaction—how learning is defined, its purpose, what is most important, the learner's role—incorporates the educator's perspective on race and culture and how (or whether) it should come into play during the learning transaction. Educators who are of color tend to be more conscious of the difference that race or ethnicity might make in any learning transaction than those who are not (Harlow, 2003). White educators may tend to think only about their own race when they teach a course on multiculturalism or race.

Learner's Perception of the Learning Transaction. The learner's perception of the nature of the learning transaction, its purpose, and possible outcome is filtered through his or her experiences, some of which are based on race and culture. For example, a personal friend who was schooled in Jamaica entered Columbia University and based her knowledge of how to behave in a university classroom on a very formal relationship between instructor and student. So formal was the system she hailed from that when the instructor entered her college classroom she stood up. Whenever she was called on to answer a question, she stood up. Finally, an African American classmate took her aside and questioned her unnecessary deference to a White instructor. The African American student's perception of the instructor–learner interaction was racialized (meaning that the experience was interpreted through a racial lens); my friend's perception of the relationship was drawn from her past experience where race was not as salient.

Content and Context. Roberson, Kulik, and Pepper (2009) posited that learner motivation might be affected by the racially differentiated learners' perception of the content and the context. Specifically, in their study they proposed that because non-Whites were more likely to have experienced discrimination and therefore have more to benefit from diversity training, they would also be more motivated to use their training. Their research did in fact support that non-White participants had significantly higher transfer strategy scores than White participants. Transfer strategies included behaviors such as thinking about using the diversity skills learned or they talked with others about the skills learned. Transfer strategies are considered a precondition for learning transfer, and although Roberson et al. conflate transfer strategies and training transfer, their hypothesis is what is important when they state, "We hypothesize that this [increased use of transfer strategies among non-Whites] may occur because of greater perceived applicability and relevance of diversity training knowledge for the job" (p. 81). Furthermore, they point out an important idea regarding the perception of participants of color: If, as some research posits (Linnehan, Chrobot-Mason, & Konrad, 2006, as cited in Roberson et al.), training symbolizes what the organization *believes* [italics added] is important, then an organization's commitment of time to diversity training is an indicator of desired change. Non-White participants would have more invested in this type of change than White participants. The authors' discussion of this indicates the way in which the learner's perception of the organizational context can be linked to race, ethnicity, or culture.

Theoretical and Anecdotal Evidence for Racial or Cultural Differences Influencing Transfer

Roberson et al. (2009) is one of the very few research studies that juxtapose learning transfer with race and how race or culture might influence the process.

However, there is theoretical and anecdotal support for the premise. Sociocultural theory (Alfred, 2002) posits that learning and knowledge are interlaced with context and that learner engagement is, at least in part, a feature of cultural identity. In contrast, some might offer that in these postracial times it is better to not see color. However, others posit that color-blindness is not a solution to the issue of racism but a means to bury racial difference (Closson, 2010). From this perspective, race and racial differences are always present but frequently unspoken and unexamined.

Several adult education scholars conceptualize program planning and delivery where race and ethnicity are potential factors influencing the learning–teaching transaction. Caffarella (2002) clearly indicates that the acknowledgment of cultural difference in the planning can be an enhancement to transfer of learning. Martin (2004) alludes to this idea in his discussion of the urban context where large populations of learners from a low socioeconomic background are predominantly of color. Martin points out that the learning needs of this population should dictate the instructional approaches so that the lived experiences of learners are integrated with the content. He suggests teaching techniques that can accommodate this, such as case studies, metaphors, analogies, and the like. Sheared's (1999) "polyrhythmic realities" notes that relevance of content to work and home of learners should be key in adult basic education (ABE) programs. Her premise is that strengthening the relevance of ABE programs to learners of color might increase retention and participation of African Americans. One way to increase relevance is to dialogue with learners about how they expect to use the knowledge gained (Sheared, 1999). These learner-identified situations can then be integrated into the class. For example, in a basic education math course where a goal is for adults to count to 100, counting can easily be based on problems drawn from the learners' experiences. Adult educators may believe that all of these ideas simply represent good planning and good teaching, which they do. They may feel that learners' experiences may not differ based on race or culture, which may be true. The point is to allow the *opportunity* for possible differences to surface as opposed to assuming that there is no difference. To some extent, the ability for learners to share culturally distinct experiences will depend on how the adult educator has positioned himself or herself in terms of comfort discussing issues of culture and race. Educator positionality is discussed in the following section.

Regarding adult education in the international and nonformal education context, Closson and Kaye (2012) noted that if the educator hails from the dominant culture, it is important that the educator interact with humility and tact when working with nondominant groups in developing countries. Even in the domestic scene, Guy (1999) hypothesizes that cultural differences between the adult educator and learners have the potential to further marginalize nondominant learners. He reminds us that differences in race and class between educator and learner can lead to significant misinterpretations and misunderstandings about the learning environment. To mitigate this potential,

Guy suggests increased educator self-awareness, an examination of one's curricula and methods; his belief is that the teaching–learning transaction can be much enhanced if the educator is culturally relevant. The assumption seems to be that an enhanced transaction will result in nondominant learners taking control of their lives and improving their social condition, which is the objective of adult education from Guy's perspective. Although there are no cultural self-awareness instruments specifically for adult educators (Rhodes, 2011), the CDAI (Cultural Diversity Awareness Inventory) is a 28-item self-report questionnaire that, although developed for elementary classroom teachers, has also been used with higher education faculty. A 5-point Likert scale is used to answer items such as "I would be comfortable in settings with people who speak an English dialect different from my own" and "It is important to identify immediately the ethnic groups of the children I serve" (Rhodes, 2011, p. 10). Adult educators could use such a tool to stimulate their own self-awareness. Similar instruments exist for counselors, but only the CDAI is grounded in education.

The Center for Creative Leadership (CCL) provides some anecdotal evidence for race influencing transfer. In their African American leadership program, CCL uses same-race educators and management coaches because they believe it allows enhanced feedback absent any underlying issues of bias. Anecdotally, African American participants have reported that they are more likely to believe and thus *want* to incorporate behavior changes suggested by the trainer or the leadership coach (Ohlott, 2002). So here we find the desire to transfer learning seemingly linked to same-race coaches and trainers, although, admittedly, there is no assessment of learning transfer.

Implications for Adult Education Practitioners

What might an adult education practitioner do based on the discussion shared here? There is always the option to do nothing. Given the limited empirical evidence that any of this influences transfer, that option might seem reasonable. However, based on the significant current racial and cultural disparities that exist, it is hoped that you will not choose it. As educators, we are committed to taking every opportunity to make a positive difference through education and learning. Here are some additional options.

Consider completing a self-report like the CDAI to assess your cultural diversity awareness and include consideration of cultural and racial differences in the program planning. Any model of program planning includes some form of needs assessment. Ask questions designed to determine the racial and cultural climate of the organization or community where the learning is to be transferred. Ask about the racial and cultural demographics of the learners. In Caffarella's (2002) planning model, she advocates developing a plan specifically for learning transfer. Creating a plan for transfer can directly incorporate instructor strategies for overcoming some of the racial and cultural barriers identified in the community or organization.

Using a problem-based learning (PBL) format where problems are actually generated by the learners (which is only one type of PBL) enables individual or community problems to emerge from the context. This approach deliberately puts more control into the hands of the learners and therefore enables them to determine the extent to which their learning will be couched within issues around race or cultural differences.

The adult educator can acknowledge racial and cultural differences. Acknowledging racial and cultural differences, if handled sensibly and sensitively, can be a signal to nondominant racial and cultural groups that the educator "sees" them and is willing to become aware of and dialogue with them regarding the challenges they might face. Typically, in the literature, instructors' decision making about how, and whether, to racially position themselves (meaning to acknowledge one's own race and the fact that race or cultural difference could play a role in the learning transaction) is discussed only when the content is specifically about racism or multiculturalism—in other words, when race is legitimized by virtue of it being clearly identified as a part of the course content (Baszile, 2004). Most adult education programs do not directly address race and culture. So, in the rest of our adult education programs, how do we acknowledge racial differences? Educators can provide an opportunity for learners to identify whether race or cultural difference is of concern. One way to do this is to have learners identify their hopes and fears regarding the course and application of the knowledge and skills learned. If, through this process, the learners have not raised concerns about cultural differences or racial differences being potential barriers in the course or at the site of transfer—home, community, organization—then the educator can determine whether to raise it or not. Questions can be asked, such as: "How do you think cultural or racial differences might affect our learning in these sessions?" Or "When you are ready to apply what you learn here do you think differences in race or culture might affect your ability to use what you've learned?"

However, there are some circumstances where it is more imperative that the issue be raised directly. For example, in a program addressing job readiness skills when the learners are predominantly from nondominant groups, or a program for law enforcement officers where the racial and cultural difference among communities juxtaposed with the race of the officer may have a significant influence on how the officer conducts himself or herself. These are examples of two distinct types of circumstances where the potential for a racial dynamic at the site of transfer could significantly influence whether, and how, learning is transferred. In instances like these, during the program planning when learner needs are accounted for, racial and cultural difference should be a prominent element. Therefore, it is during the planning when the educator can deliberately include culturally resonant metaphors, case studies, and examples. It is also during this time when the educator should determine how prominent a role his or her own race should play. The next step could be to carry this forward to analyze the environment and potential barriers that may exist for learning transfer. This step is based on the possibility that community and organizational environments may be biased, too. Educators must be open to brainstorming with learners how to realistically identify and navigate such barriers.

Using culturally relevant music, drama, literature, metaphors, and analogies helps nondominant groups feel valued and should reduce potential barriers to learning. Especially in developing countries, using music, song, and storytelling is culturally appropriate, and the knowledge couched in this way is readily understood, accepted, and applied (Silver, 2001). A constellation of these types of micro-actions and behaviors can build a bond of trust between adult educator and learner.

Adult education practitioners can provide instructor support and feedback. They can accompany the learner in early attempts at demonstrating the learned skill to provide support, much like an apprenticeship. Closson and Kaye (2012) noted that learners in developing countries, especially from rural and low-income areas, should be supported via educator accompaniment and feedback in their early efforts at transferring their learning into community service. When training tutors in a spiritual development program, Closson and Kaye noted the importance of experienced tutors accompanying new tutors during their initial workshops to offer feedback and guidance, especially about levels of sensitivity to cultural difference. CCL, as was mentioned earlier, uses African American feedback coaches in their African American Leadership program. These coaches can supply objective feedback based on psychological instrumentation, which is part and parcel of all CCL's leadership training, and can share their own personal stories of challenges perceived as emanating from racially charged environments.

What Are the Risks of Using Any of These Approaches?

A primary risk is that learners may misperceive your purpose and misconstrue your words. If we are a nation of cowards (Holder, 2009) when it comes to racial dialogue, it is at least in part because cross-racial communication is so often misperceived (Patton & Catching, 2009). So a primary risk in raising issues of racial, cultural, and ethnic differences is that learners may not immediately think that your efforts are a means of enhancing the transfer of the concepts and skills you are teaching. They may misconstrue your words and, at the very worst, conceive your efforts as racist. The premise on which I base this statement is that, especially in the United States, not to talk about race, not to recognize racial or cultural difference is the appreciated norm. Unfortunately, there is no guaranteed way to rectify this problem. Adult education practitioners will make this decision on their own based on their level of comfort and personal assessment of importance of the issue.

References

Alfred, M. (2002). The promise of sociocultural theory in democratizing adult education. In M. Alfred (Ed.), *New Directions For Adult and Continuing Education: No. 96. Learning and sociocultural contexts: Implications for adults, community, and workplace education* (pp. 3–13). San Francisco, CA: Jossey-Bass. doi: 10.1002/ace.74

Baldwin, T., & Ford, J. (1988). Transfer of training: A review and directions for future research. *Personnel Psychology, 41*(65), 63–105.

Baszile, D. 2004. "Who does she think she is?" Growing up nationalist and ending up teaching race in White space. In D. Cleveland (Ed.), *A long way to go: Conversations about race by African-American faculty and graduate students* (pp. 158–170). New York, NY: Lang.

Caffarella, R. (2002). *Planning programs for adult learners.* San Francisco, CA: Jossey-Bass.

Closson, R. (2010). Critical race theory and adult education. *Adult Education Quarterly, 60*(3), 261–283.

Closson, R., & Kaye, S. (2012). Learning by doing: Preparation of Baha'i nonformal tutors. In P. Isaac (Ed.), *New Directions For Adult and Continuing Education: No. 133. Expanding the boundaries of adult religious education: Strategies, techniques, and partnerships for the new millennium* (pp. 45–57). San Francisco, CA: Jossey-Bass. doi: 10.1002/ace.20006

Guy, T. (1999). Culture as context for adult education: The need for culturally relevant adult education. In T. Guy (Ed.), *New Directions for Adult and Continuing Education: No. 82. Providing culturally relevant adult education* (pp. 5–18). San Francisco, CA: Jossey-Bass. doi: 10.1002/ace.8201

Haney Lopez, I. (1994). The social construction of race: Some observations on illusion, fabrication, and choice. *Harvard Civil Rights—Civil Liberties Law Review, 29*(1), 1–53.

Harlow, R. (2003). "Race doesn't matter, But …": The effect of race on professor's experiences and emotion management in the undergraduate college classroom. *Social Psychology Quarterly, 66*(4), 348–363.

Holder, E. (2009). *Attorney General Eric Holder at the Department of Justice African American History Month program.* Washington, DC: United States Department of Justice. Retrieved from http://www.justice.gov/ag/speeches/2009/ag-speech-090218.html

Kochhar, R., Fry, R., & Taylor, P. (2011). *Wealth gaps rise to record highs between Whites, Blacks and Hispanics.* Retrieved from http://pewresearch.org/pubs/2069/housing-bubble-subprime-mortgages-hispanics-blacks-household-wealth-disparity

Martin, L. (2004). Adult education in the urban context. In L. Martin & E. Rogers (Eds.), *New Directions for Adult and Continuing Education: No. 101. Adult education in an urban context* (pp. 3–16). San Francisco, CA: Jossey-Bass. doi: 10.1002/ace.124

Ohlott, P. (2002). Myths versus realities of single-identity leadership development. *Training & Development, 56*(11), 32–37.

Patton, L., & Catching, C. (2009). Teaching while Black: Narratives of African-American student affairs faculty. *International Journal of Qualitative Studies in Education, 22*(6), 713–728. doi: 10.1080/09518390903333897

Pratt, D. (1998). *Five perspectives on teaching in adult and higher education.* Malabar, FL: Krieger.

Rhodes, C. (2011). *Descriptive study of culturally responsive teaching practices of adult education ESOL teachers.* Unpublished manuscript.

Roberson, L., Kulik, C. T., & Pepper, M. B. (2009). Individual and environmental factors influencing the use of transfer strategies after diversity training. *Group & Organizational Management, 34*(1), 67–89. doi: 10.1177/1059601108329732

Sheared, V. (1999). Giving voice: Inclusion of African American students' polyrhythmic realities in adult basic education. In T. Guy (Ed.), *New Directions for Adult and Continuing Education: No. 82. Providing culturally relevant adult education* (pp. 33–48). San Francisco, CA: Jossey-Bass. doi: 10.1002/ace.8203

Silver, D. (2001). Songs and storytelling: Bringing health messages to life in Uganda. *Education for Health, 14*(1), 51–60. doi:10.1080/13576280010015362

United States Department of Labor (2010). *Bureau of labor statistics unemployment rates by race and ethnicity* [Data file]. Retrieved from http://www.bls.gov/opub/ted/2011/ted_20111005.htm

ROSEMARY CLOSSON, PhD, is an associate professor at the University of South Florida.

New Directions for Adult and Continuing Education • DOI: 10.1002/ace

7

This chapter approaches transfer from the perspective of supporting learners implementing personal change based on their learning experiences. Models of transition and change are presented and discussed, including aspects of resistance to and facilitation of change.

Understanding Transfer as Personal Change: Concerns, Intentions, and Resistance

Jeani C. Young

> Learning, by definition, involves change. It requires us to explore new ideas, acquire new skills, develop new ways of understanding old experiences, and so on. No one is the same after learning something.
>
> —Brookfield, 2006, p. 214

Adult education is about change. Change in knowledge and understanding. Change in attitudes and beliefs. Change in skills and behaviors. The transfer that adult educators and learners often want to achieve is that change. In situations where transfer equals change, models of change can be useful to describe, support, and predict transfer. In this chapter, we will investigate two change models and how they can be helpful to adult educators.

In *Learning in Adulthood*, Merriam, Caffarella, and Baumgartner (2006) define learning as "a process that brings together cognitive, emotional and environmental influences and experiences for acquiring, enhancing and *making changes* in one's knowledge, skills, values and worldviews" (p. 48, emphasis added). The literature on transformative learning is devoted to understanding and teaching for significant change: "a deep shift in perspective during which habits of mind become more open, more permeable, and better justified" (Cranton & Taylor, 2012, p. 201).

When we talk about adult education, we are often talking about programs, courses, or one-on-one consultations that encourage and support individual change. At times, intended change is explicit as in programs to assist

New Directions for Adult and Continuing Education, no. 137, Spring 2013 © 2013 Wiley Periodicals, Inc.
Published online in Wiley Online Library (wileyonlinelibrary.com) • DOI: 10.1002/ace.20046

participants improve self-esteem or self-concept, or explore possible selves (Rossiter, 2007). At other times, the change is implied as in programs addressing issues such as parenting, workplace diversity, or management of health issues. Tennant (2000) explains that changes commonly involve the reorienting of attitudes, values, and beliefs and the way individuals understand their roles in different contexts.

Adult Education and Change

Continuing professional education, literacy, numeracy, job search skills, diabetes management, and smoking cessation programs are diverse in content and context but have in common the intent of change. Learners come to these programs seeking help and guidance in making changes in their lives. When learners take what they gain from adult education programs and apply it—*transfer it*—to their own lives, there is change. This change occurs in individual learners, their context, and their learning. If we agree that learning is an ongoing, situated process that does not end when the learner leaves the classroom, workshop, or other educational setting, then it is easy to see the need to view transfer as a fluid rather than static concept (Hager & Hodkinson, 2009). In fact, Hager and Hodkinson (2009) recommend reconstructing the concept of learning transfer as "learning as becoming within a transitional process of boundary crossing" (p. 635). For purposes of this chapter, the concepts of transition, implementation, and change will all be used to describe aspects of learners' experiences as they move into and out of adult education contexts as part of their ongoing growth and development.

At this point it is helpful to look a bit closer at the concept of transition. In a sociocultural context, individuals are always interacting with their surroundings. Beach (1999) describes it as the recursive interaction of learners and social organizations in mutual relationship over time. Any continuity or transformation of attitude, belief, skill, or knowledge is contextualized and embedded in place and time to some degree. Learners rely on culturally developed and shared signs and symbols such as technology and language use (including jargon, technical terminology, or local connotative meanings) to make sense of the context and of what is expected of them.

In adult and continuing education, the experience of moving from an educational setting into a related work or leisure setting is normally an expected one. Adults normally participate in educational programs because they are applicable to their career, job, or other interests such as health or leisure activities. As such, it is often easier for the learners to make that transition, as they can hold their identity as a worker, a parent, a diabetic, a glassblower, and so on, as they participate in educational activities and reflect on how the activities and the role relate. The two settings may also share the same or very similar language, technology, and assumptions—for example, workplace training on a new computer system, continuing medical education for physicians, or workshops on advanced gardening techniques for avid home gardeners. However, learners approaching educational activities exclusively focused on their role as a student have less impetus to engage in critical reflection related to life away from the classroom, which in turn makes transition, when it occurs, more challenging.

For adult learners to maintain continuity of a newly learned skill such as arithmetic from a classroom to a shopping trip requires them to first recognize the application of the skill in the new context. It may be more difficult for learners in an adult basic education class who see themselves as "students" in the classroom but as workers, parents, volunteers, and so on, away from the classroom to see the opportunities for application. When they do recognize the opportunity to use what they have learned, they then may need to transform the manipulation of numbers from the structured way they practiced in the classroom to informal and self-directed actions in a distracting environment. They also have to believe that taking the time to change their behavior, from "guesstimating" if they have enough money for their purchases to actually adding things up, benefits them enough to make the effort. Beach (1999) termed this type of change a *consequential transition*—a change in the relationship between the learner and the social activities in context. This may occur through a change in the learner or the activity or both, and normally involves conscious reflection and the trying on of possible selves—a person's conception or mental image of a future version of himself or herself, which could be idealized or anticipated (Rossiter, 2007). In this case, the learner would be trying the possible self of one who "figures while he or she shops."

Two types of consequential transitions that Beach (1999) proposes are particularly relevant here. The first, "collateral transition," is a nonlinear transition that is negotiated through simultaneous participation in multiple communities. An example would be a person participating in religious education prior to marriage to someone of a different faith. That person would negotiate his or her identity as a member of each religious community simultaneously as his or her beliefs about each developed. The shopper in the paragraph above is simultaneously participating in learning arithmetic in one setting and using arithmetic in another. Each activity influences learning and how the shopper interacts with the two settings.

The second type of transition is an "encompassing transition," which occurs within the bounds of one community. This transition is also generally linear and unidirectional along the line of the desired change. Examples would include beginning a new job and learning the skills and knowledge necessary to participate fully or transitions related to organizational or departmental shifts such as implementation of new technology or policies. In-house training and professional development would be considered encompassing transitions. Both types of transitions share a focus on construction of knowledge, identities, skills, and beliefs as opposed to simple application of a skill or procedure.

As an adult educator, you may be more used to thinking about what you do in terms of learning objectives, course goals, or test grades than in terms of transition and change. There are many models of change that offer useful frameworks, especially if your educational programs are supporting a larger organizational change. As working within larger change movements is the exception rather than the rule, the remainder of this chapter will focus on two models that emphasize personal change: the concerns-based adoption model and the theory of planned behavior.

Concerns-Based Adoption Model (CBAM)

When thinking about programs where transfer of learning involves implementing change, it can help to have a more detailed description of what change looks like. The concerns-based adoption model (CBAM) conceptualizes change as a "developmental process in attitudes and behaviors for individuals attempting to put new ideas and practices into use" (Anderson, 2009, p. 65). It also provides a set of assumptions about change, a way of describing what the implementation of change looks like, and a taxonomy for the concerns individuals may have about the change.

CBAM is based on the assumptions that change occurs over time, is the work of individuals, is highly personal, involves development in skills and attitude, and can be facilitated (Anderson, 2009). Researchers at the University of Texas developed the CBAM in the late 1970s and early 1980s based on those assumptions, to describe and evaluate K–12 teachers' experiences of educational change. However, it is also applicable to individuals involved in formal adult education programs, continuing professional development, or ongoing consultations for behavior or attitude change (Grol, Bosch, Hulscher, Eccles, & Wensing, 2007). Along the lines of the original research, teachers of adults or children participating in professional development will learn about new approaches and strategies that they want to implement in their classrooms. But how often do we attend a session or a class and then, upon returning to our regular context, have concerns about implementation? These concerns tend to fall into three categories: self concerns, task concerns, and impact concerns.

CBAM divides these concerns into a developmental series of stages (stages of concern) and pairs them with common levels of implementation, which they term *levels of use*. Table 7.1 shows the stages and levels as described by the model.

All levels of concern involve attitudes, feelings, and motivations about implementing the change. The type of concern tends to vary based on the level of commitment to the change and the level of implementation of the change. For our purposes here, the stages of awareness and informational concerns are less applicable. These concerns center on information seeking that would be addressed by the educational course or program the learner has completed or is currently attending.

New Directions for Adult and Continuing Education • DOI: 10.1002/ace

Table 7.1. Stages of Concern, Types of Concern, and Levels of Use.

Stages of Concern	Types of Concerns	Levels of Use
Awareness		None
Informational	Self Concerns	Orientation
Personal		Preparation
Management	Task Concerns	Mechanical
Consequence		Routine/Refinement
Collaboration	Impact Concerns	Integration
Refocusing		Renewal

The key concerns emerging from a professional development or training program or an initial round of consultations tend to center around personal, management, and consequence concerns. Learners may have personal concerns including worrying about their ability to carry out the necessary actions to make the change happen in their context, whether it is a change that they really want to make, or whether they have the personal, emotional, and physical resources to make the change happen. For example, an English language learner in a beginning-level class may be anxious about speaking English in a nonclass setting such as a doctor's office. A participant in a diabetes management course may question whether the dietary changes are really worth the effort. A counselor attending continuing professional education on new government regulations regarding billing and Medicare may have concerns about completing all the paperwork accurately. Management concerns tend to develop when learners have had some time to work with the new behaviors, skills, or attitudes. They can become anxious about time commitments, logistics, organization, and prioritizing responsibilities (Bailey & Palsha, 1992). In the original model focusing on K–12 teachers, consequence concerns referred to impact of the change on students. Generally speaking, consequence concerns would relate to the impact of the change on the context and the other people involved such as clients, patients, customers, coworkers, family members, and so on.

Levels of use are based on the knowledge that implementation of change is rarely an all-or-nothing proposition. Implementation may be partial and may take some time to accomplish. Levels of use are generic concepts as the details of each situation vary. For our purposes here, the levels of preparation, mechanical, and routine or refinement are the most applicable. The preparation level refers to learners who have committed to making a change and are readying themselves to begin. The mechanical level includes learners who are focused mainly on everyday use as they work to routinize the tasks and master the skills needed. Implementation at this point can be superficial and unreflective (Hall & Loucks, 1977). Learners continue at this level until the activities surrounding the change are stable and routine. The routine or refinement level builds on the routine established in the previous level, and the learner is comfortable enough to begin to look more closely at impacts on the setting and others involved. Additional changes may be made to improve the situation, either alone or with colleagues or other peers. These levels and stages imply a stepwise development to successful completion of all levels; however, realistically, researchers found that many participants will not reach the seventh stage and may plateau at the routine stage (Anderson, 1997).

Two other aspects of CBAM add to the understanding of transitions involving implementation of change. The first is innovation configuration (Anderson, 1997). Innovation configuration recognizes that even in the same context, change may not look the same when implemented by different people. An innovation profile can be developed describing important behaviors or attitudes supporting the change and possible variations on the theme. Second, and more important here, is the concept of the change facilitator. The ways in which change is implemented can vary widely even given the same professional development opportunities. In situations where the learner is engaged in a collateral transition, continuing to interact with the educational and application contexts over a period of time, the adult educator can act as a change facilitator. One of the change facilitator's roles in CBAM is to link the application setting (be it work, leisure, home, etc.) to an external "resource setting." In the original model, the change facilitator would be in the teacher's work setting linking them to external resources; however, in the context of adult education, it is just as likely that the adult educator acting as a change facilitator would be in the "resource setting" instead.

In the case of the participant in a diabetes management course, the participant may have both self and task concerns as he or she moves from preparation into the mechanical level of use. The diabetes educator needs to share the same view of the innovation configuration, and it is likely that the educator will have many resources on healthy eating and glucose monitoring. As a change facilitator, the diabetes educator would ensure that the resources were clearly linked to the participant's application setting (i.e., healthy eating resources using images of the inside of a model refrigerator or pantry, eating-out guides that list actual menu items from popular restaurants, glucose monitoring "cheat sheets" using images of the monitor supplied by the educational program, etc.). As much as you plan, there will always be unexpected situations and concerns when implementing change. Incorporating a model of occasional follow-up sessions or other continuing communication options over the ensuing months would allow the participant to have access to ongoing support and resources as new questions and challenges arise.

Theory of Planned Behavior (TPB)

The second model describes one way of looking at motivations to implement learning. The theory of planned behavior (TPB) focuses on the learner's intentions and the personal and contextual factors that influence those intentions.

(Ajzen, 1991). TPB has frequently been used to study changes made by individuals following consultations or workshops on health issues, nutrition, substance abuse, weight loss, physical activity, and technology among other areas (Armitage & Conner, 2001; Casper, 2007; Wiethoff, 2004).

The basic theory breaks down into three major components: beliefs and attitudes about the behavior; normative beliefs and perceived social pressure; and perceived behavioral control. Beliefs about the behavior refer to whether the learners believe that applying what they have learned in a particular way will help them to meet their goal. If one of the goals in a job search workshop is for the participants to use social media as part of their job search strategy, do they believe that using social media will improve their chances of getting a job? Attitudes toward the behavior include beliefs and other aspects of the behavior that encourage the learner to view the action favorably or unfavorably such as anticipated emotions and benefits (Ajzen, 2011). Does the participant think using social media will be enjoyable or frustrating? Interesting or boring? Providing opportunities for critical reflection on underlying beliefs and attitudes can help clarify issues or work through emotional responses that may be blocking intentions to change.

Normative beliefs refer to what the learner thinks "everyone else" thinks about the behavior. Beliefs about colleague, supervisor, and classmate opinions may or may not be accurate, but the learner's perception of those beliefs affect the amount and direction of social pressure he or she feels about the behavior. Does our job seeker's primary peer group approve or disapprove of social media in general? Providing safe opportunities to explore class opinion or practice talking with family or peers about their beliefs can assist learners in confirming or updating their perceptions of the social climate surrounding the change.

The third component is perceived behavioral control. This includes the individual's perception of how easy or difficult the behavior is. Note that this does not necessarily reflect any objective measure of difficulty. For a smoker, not buying a pack of cigarettes is far more difficult than an objective measure of the effort to go to a store and make a purchase would indicate. This component also includes perceived obstacles such as lack of resources, access, or time to implement the behavior. A "reality check" regarding objective obstacles can be useful to learners, especially when combined with brainstorming about additional sources of resources and support.

While Ajzen (1991) considers perceived behavioral control to be interchangeable with self-efficacy, studies conducted using TPB have found self-efficacy to be a related but separate component with predictive value of its own (Armitage & Conner, 2001; Conner & Armitage, 1998). As Connor and Armitage (1998) describe it, "People intend to engage in behaviors of which they feel they are capable" (p. 1439). Something may be perceived as difficult, but if learners have high self-efficacy, then they may believe that they are quite capable of meeting the challenge. This appears to be especially likely in situations involving academic change such as implementing new study strategies

Figure 7.1. A Modified Version of the Theory of Planned Behavior.

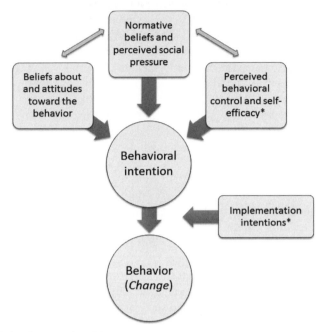

*Not included in the original model.

or improving effectiveness in searching library databases as these activities rely more on skills and resources than control over behavior. Figure 7.1 shows a modified version of the TPB, including the additional elements of self-efficacy and implementation intentions.

All three of these components influence each other as well as influence the behavioral intention. The intention captures the motivation and decision to exert effort to implement the behavior. Given the personal attitude toward social media, the perceived pressure from various sources (peers, media, career counselor, etc.) to use or not use social media, and the perception of how hard or easy it will be combined with self-efficacy regarding computer use, will our job seeker decide to use social media in his or her job search? Will our job seeker form an intention to take what he or she learned about using social media and act on it? Research has shown that individuals with active behavioral intentions are significantly more likely to follow through on the behavior than those who do not (Armitage & Conner, 2001).

Two factors can influence this probability—strength of the intention and implementation intentions. Obviously if the intention is strong the person is even more likely to follow through. However, even if the intention is moderate, the addition of implementation intentions can support individuals in following through with their plan (Gollwitzer, 1999; Orbeil, Hodgldns, & Sheeran,

1997). Gollwitzer (1999) describes implementation intentions as specifying the when, where, and how of the behavior. They clarify context and actions and "link anticipated opportunities with goal-directed responses . . . [and] the person commits himself or herself to respond to a certain situation in a specific manner" (p. 494) which, in turn, can support automation of action.

Leaving a workshop on creative writing with new resources and ideas and the intention to do something with it all does not necessarily mean that something productive will be done. Implementation intentions are useful to attract attention to opportunities to act (getting started) as well as to support motivation to continue acting (persistence). An implementation intention would be "when I drink my morning coffee, I will write at least two things down in my idea journal." It specifies a context that provides a situational cue paired with a goal-directed action. When faced with attractive alternatives, implementation intentions can also be used to keep on task. "When I am writing, I will turn off e-mail" would be an example of a distraction-inhibiting implementation intention.

When Learners Resist Change

What happens when learners refuse or resist change? It is not uncommon to have participants in classes and workshops disengage, either mentally or physically, especially in situations where their participation is required by an external entity. How can these models help us think about resistance in a different way? Brookfield (2006) suggests that learners can resist for a wide range of reasons including perceived irrelevance of the content, low self-efficacy as a learner, or dislike of the instructor. The reason that comes into play here is fear of change. The continuation of the quote at the beginning of this chapter describes it well: "The change might not be very dramatic or even evident. But even incremental and imperceptible change carries its own discomforts" (p. 214).

Piaget divided learning into two major types, assimilative and accommodative (Lemme, 2005). Assimilative learning is what Atherton (1999) terms *additive* learning—it simply adds to your current understanding and supports your view of how things are and how they work. Accommodative learning is what Atherton terms *supplantive* learning—it supplants or replaces (in whole or part) something you had previously learned. Supplantive learning tends to be resisted. This is especially true in cases where there is significant emotional investment in the learner's current understandings and beliefs. Dufresne (2006) tells of an instructor who systematically refused to go to professional development workshops because "she knew what she was doing and *the workshops disturbed her*" (p. 348, emphasis added). She refused to attend any workshop that offered new ideas that might make her doubt what she was currently doing and challenge her underlying assumptions about teaching and learning.

Participants in situations where the boundaries of their beliefs and assumptions are challenged are likely to have personal concerns and negative attitudes about the behavior accompanying the change. Some participants may not understand their reaction to the situation as resistance to challenge. Atherton (1999) describes the cognitive response to the challenge of supplantive learning as confusion and disorientation, a not-able-to-wrap-my-brain-around-it feeling that they could not put their finger on. It can occur as part of a larger role change (such as nondiabetic to diabetic or employee to unemployed job seeker) that adult education is attempting to support. Alternatively, it can creep up on individuals as they begin to work with content and some concepts collide with internal walls of belief. Emotional responses vary based on the individual's temperament and the strength of his or her attachment to current beliefs and can range from sadness to irritation to anger consistent with reactions to loss.

In a previous section there is an example of a counselor attending continuing professional education on new government regulations regarding billing and Medicare and the potential issues at the personal stage of concern. The counselor's concerns about completing all the paperwork accurately may partially stem from a strong belief that he or she is a "people person" and not a "detail person." This belief can influence self-efficacy and attitude regarding the required change. The counselor may resist the change by "tuning out" of the workshop on the new regulations, which could leave him or her ill-prepared to provide needed documentation for clients. The counselor may be confused about the procedure and show frustration with the new forms and complain about their "unnecessary complexity" to the instructor and other participants.

When a learner is confused and disoriented, it is important for the instructor to take this opportunity to work through the resistance and support learning while mitigating the loss of the supplanted understanding as much as possible. Using the TPB model, the instructor could help by respecting the learner's concerns, sensitively leveraging normative beliefs, supporting skill building for increased self-efficacy, and, if possible, analyzing the application setting to gain more accurate perceptions of behavioral control.

Conclusion

The theme throughout this chapter has been supporting learners implementing personal change based on their learning experiences. Choosing to look at the concept of transfer not simply as application of knowledge in a different context opens up a different perspective on the causes of transfer problems as well as potential support for learners in these situations. Do the learners perceive that the application setting affords them the opportunity and resources to productively implement the change? How does the relationship between the learner and both the learning setting and the application setting develop as they transition between the settings and how does that affect the change?

Whether the change is small or transformative, whether the transition is collateral or encompassing, the models presented here can provide a starting

dissertation

point for considering alternate approaches. For further exploration, sociocultural approaches to transfer take into account changing social situations and the individual learner's multidirectional movement from one organization and situation to another (Tuomi-Gröhn & Engeström, 2003). Related work on boundary-crossing highlighting the individual's "ability to function competently in multiple contexts" (Walker, 2007, p. 178) and work on possible selves (Rossiter, 2007) can also add to this discussion.

References

Ajzen, I. (1991). The theory of planned behavior. *Organizational Behavior and Human Decision Processes, 50*(2), 179–211.

Ajzen, I. (2011). The theory of planned behaviour: Reactions and reflections. *Psychology and Health, 26*(9), 1113–1127.

Anderson, S. E. (1997). Understanding teacher change: Revisiting the concerns based adoption model. *Curriculum Inquiry, 27*(3), 331–367.

Anderson, S. E. (2009). Moving change: Evolutionary perspectives on educational change. In A. Hargreaves, A. Lieberman, M. Fullan, & D. Hopkins (Eds.), *Second international handbook of educational change* (pp. 65–84). New York, NY: Springer.

Armitage, C. J., & Conner, M. (2001). Efficacy of the theory of planned behaviour: A meta-analytic review. *British Journal of Social Psychology, 40*(4), 471–499.

Atherton, J. (1999). Resistance to learning: A discussion based on participants in in-service professional training programmes. *Journal of Vocational Education and Training, 51*(1), 77–90.

Bailey, D. B., & Palsha, S. A. (1992). Qualities of the stages of concern questionnaire and implications for educational innovations. *Journal of Educational Research, 85*(4), 226–232.

Beach, K. (1999). Consequential transitions: A sociocultural expedition beyond transfer in education. *Review of Research in Education, 24*, 101–139. doi: 10.2307/1167268

Brookfield, S. (2006). *The skillful teacher: On technique, trust, and responsiveness in the classroom.* San Francisco, CA: Jossey-Bass.

Casper, E. S. (2007). The theory of planned behavior applied to continuing education for mental health professionals. *Psychiatric Services, 58*(10), 1324–1329. doi: 10.1176/appi.ps.58.10.1324

Conner, M., & Armitage, C. J. (1998). Extending the theory of planned behavior: A review and avenues for further research. *Journal of Applied Social Psychology, 28*(15), 1429–1464.

Cranton, P., & Taylor, E. W. (2012). Transformative learning. In P. Jarvis & M. Watts (Eds.), *The Routledge international handbook of learning* (pp. 194–204). New York, NY: Routledge.

Dufresne, T. (2006). Exploring the processes in becoming biliterate: The roles of resistance to learning and affect. *International Journal of Learning, 12*(8), 347–354.

Gollwitzer, P. M. (1999). Implementation intentions: Strong effects of simple plans. *American Psychologist, 54*(7), 493–503.

Grol, R. P. T. M., Bosch, M. C., Hulscher, M. E. J. L., Eccles, M. P., & Wensing, M. (2007). Planning and studying improvement in patient care: The use of theoretical perspectives. *Milbank Quarterly, 85*(1), 93–138. doi:10.1111/j.1468-0009.2007.00478.x

Hager, P., & Hodkinson, P. (2009). Moving beyond the metaphor of transfer of learning. *British Educational Research Journal, 35*(4), 619–638.

Hall, G. E., & Loucks, S. F. (1977). A developmental model for determining whether the treatment is actually implemented. *American Educational Research Journal, 14*(3), 263–276. doi: 10.2307/1162291

Lemme, B. H. (2005). *Development in adulthood* (4th ed.). Boston, MA: Allyn & Bacon.

Merriam, S. B., Caffarella, R. S., & Baumgartner, L. M. (2006). *Learning in adulthood: A comprehensive guide* (3rd ed). San Francisco, CA: Jossey-Bass.

Orbeil, S., Hodgldns, S., & Sheeran, P. (1997). Implementation intentions and the theory of planned behavior. *Personality and Social Psychology Bulletin, 23*(9), 945–954. doi: 10.1177/0146167297239004

Rossiter, M. (2007). Possible selves: An adult education perspective. In M. Rossiter (Ed.), *New Directions for Adult and Continuing Education: No. 114. Possible selves and adult learning: Perspectives and potential* (pp. 5–15). San Francisco, CA: Jossey-Bass.

Tennant, M. (2000). Adult learning for self-development and change. In A. L. Wilson & E. R. Hayes (Eds.), *Handbook of adult and continuing education* (pp. 87–100). San Francisco, CA: Jossey-Bass.

Tuomi-Gröhn, T., & Engeström, Y. (2003). *Between school and work: New perspectives on transfer and boundary-crossing.* London, England: Emerald Group.

Walker, D. (2007). Boundary-crossing competence: Theoretical considerations and educational design. *Mind, Culture, and Activity, 14*(3), 178–195.

Wiethoff, C. (2004). Motivation to learn and diversity training: Application of the theory of planned behavior. *Human Resource Development Quarterly, 15*(3), 263–278. doi: 10.1002/hrdq.1103

JEANI C. YOUNG is a lecturer in adult education and a doctoral candidate in educational psychology in the School of Education at Indiana University, Bloomington.

8

This chapter offers a practical framework for applying the learning transfer concepts discussed in this issue from a facilitation and instructional design standpoint.

Applying Transfer in Practice

Karen Kaminski, Jeffrey M. Foley, Leann M. R. Kaiser

Throughout the chapters in this issue, the authors have cited various definitions for learning transfer. For educators, in its simplest form, transfer of learning occurs when students put to practical use the knowledge and skills they gained in the classroom (near transfer). Chapter 1 defines near transfer and then goes into detail on the levels and variations of transfer beyond this. You may have read this volume cover to cover, or you may have followed our advice and read the first chapter, then the one that caught your attention, and now this chapter. Whichever your process, we are ready to practice.

Near Transfer

The first application of knowledge and skills often occurs when learners leave the classroom and return to their work or life environment. The setting is very similar if not identical to that presented in the classroom. For example, I might attend a workshop on how to make an apple pie. When I get home, the next time I have the opportunity, I follow the steps I learned precisely and my apple pie turns out pretty good. I repeat this and, with practice, the fifth pie I bake I am ready to share with company.

Think back on the chapter(s) you read. What caught your eye and enticed you to apply it the next time you facilitate a workshop or class? Perhaps you want to spend time helping students activate prior learning or related knowledge and skills to help them tie new learning to existing schema (Chapter 1). Before you get too busy with other things, make some notes on how you plan to integrate the particular techniques you choose into a lesson to enhance the likelihood that your students will transfer the learning from the classroom. Pick a class and content you are familiar with and that is perhaps closely related to the example provided in the chapter. Apply the

NEW DIRECTIONS FOR ADULT AND CONTINUING EDUCATION, no. 137, Spring 2013 © 2013 Wiley Periodicals, Inc.
Published online in Wiley Online Library (wileyonlinelibrary.com) • DOI: 10.1002/ace.20047

technique and reflect on your experience, the experience of the learners, and whether it made a difference.

Not-So-Near Transfer

As recommended to enhance transfer, the next step is to practice applying the knowledge and skills to a different setting. Now that I have learned to bake a great apple pie, I am ready to apply the same concepts to baking a peach pie. There is much similarity, but peaches are much softer and juicier than apples. I may have to practice again until I perfect the peach pie.

A good way for you to experience this is to use those same techniques you selected for near transfer and try them in a different class or in a slightly different context. In this example, you would now try activating schema with a more challenging topic, something that is not easily related to your learners' existing knowledge and skills. Help them make the connections. Do you experience the same results? Do you need to modify the process slightly? Take time to reflect on how this is going.

Farther Transfer

I might not be ready to take my pies to the fair, but I am pretty pleased with myself. I have gained quite a few skills, such as how different amounts of ingredients will affect the flavor of my pie, how long I need to bake it, and so on. My friend calls and she is planning a neighborhood gathering. She has heard through the grapevine that I make great desserts and wants to know if I can bring enough cupcakes to feed 100 people. I hesitate and decide "what the heck, it can't be that hard." I can follow a recipe; I know what happens if the oven is too hot and how to set things out to cool. I think about how I can apply what I know from baking pies (transfer my prior learning) to baking 100 cupcakes (to a new setting).

In your example, now that you are comfortable incorporating learning transfer techniques into your existing instruction, the next step might be to develop a new course or workshop from scratch. This would allow you to build in the unique aspects you want to include to enhance the likelihood for your students to transfer learning to new settings.

Intentionally Building Transfer in Instructional Design

Following an instructional design model will help you in each step of the creation of your course (Merriam & Leahy, 2005). A typical instructional design process starts with a needs assessment, attaining stakeholder buy-in and input, audience analysis, developing learning outcomes, assessment of learning or evaluation, creating the curriculum, and developing learning resources

(Gustafson & Branch, 2002). Frequently in the instructional design process, learning transfer is an afterthought. Instead, learning transfer needs to be considered at each step in the design process.

Learning Transfer and the Needs Assessment. We develop instruction to fill a gap between what is and what should be in individual knowledge and skills or performance in the workplace, home, or community environment. When conducting a needs assessment, you want to first determine that instruction is the appropriate approach to fill the gap, rather than faulty equipment or an oppressive environment. You can gain much information from asking some simple questions to set the foundation for the learning activities.

A needs assessment allows the designer to determine:

- If instruction is the best method to address the "need" or gap
- If there are any apparent barriers to transfer
- Strategies to address any needed changes or improvements to the work environment to enhance transfer
- The overall course goals

Here, we can determine if the environment is supportive of transfer, and, if not, recommend changes up front or address the challenges within the instruction.

Learning Transfer and Attaining Stakeholder Input and Buy-In. Stakeholders are individuals who have a vested interest in the outcomes of the instruction being delivered. Typical stakeholders include granting agencies, management, potential employers, and community members. The designer of the instruction wants to ensure stakeholder input and buy-in so that:

- The climate of the workplace is conducive to transfer.
- The resources being expended on learning have the highest potential for return on investment.
- The knowledge and skills desired and, hence, gained are the most accurate and current.
- There is a strong philosophical alignment between the designer and the stakeholder prior to developing the learning outcomes.

Remember, the learners or trainees are also stakeholders. If they do not identify a need or a value for the knowledge or skill, they may disengage prior to entering the learning situation. This can be one of the greatest barriers to transfer. Consider how many employees return from a training or course and report, "That was a complete waste of time—I did not learn anything." Understanding this barrier can be critical to learning transfer (Baldwin & Ford, 1988).

Audience Analysis. In the audience analysis, you may talk with or survey the learners to determine the current status of their knowledge, skills, attitude, and barriers in relation to the intended overall goals of the learning (Dick, Carey, & Carey, 2009). A thorough audience analysis increases learning transfer by helping ensure that the designer creates a learning environment and instructional materials that support learning, retention, and application (Broad, 1997; Ford & Weissbein, 1997). A good audience analysis increases learning transfer by ensuring that the designer has the most accurate picture of where the learners are in their development and where they need to go, and provides some insight into how to get there. It also provides valuable information about the learners' prior experience to allow you to activate a schema to enhance learning.

An audience analysis allows the designer to determine:

- Who the learners are (age, educational background, social makeup, prior experience)
- In what environment and context will the learner apply the learning
- The current knowledge and skill level of the learners
- Whether there are any evident or historical barriers to learning that can be addressed in the design process

Identifying barriers to learning (Merriam & Leahy, 2005) and the state of the transfer climate (Holton, Bates, & Ruona, 2000) in the audience analysis and needs assessment allows the designer to address any issues in the design process, thus increasing learning transfer.

Learning Transfer and Learning Outcomes. Learning outcomes are statements that define what the learner should be able to do after completion of the learning event. This is one of the most critical steps in the design process to help ensure learning transfer. Tips for writing learning outcomes include:

- Integrate the information learned from the needs assessment, audience analysis, and stakeholder input processes when writing the learning outcomes
- Consider using Bloom's Taxonomy when writing learning outcomes
- Write toward the potential application areas of the learning, not just toward the experience in the learning session
- Ensure that they are achievable within the instructional time frame

Good learning outcomes drive the instruction. For example, if you want the learners to be able to perform a task, then you need to give them the opportunity to observe and practice, not just tell them how. Learning outcomes promote good assessment, which supports transfer of learning. Consider cocreating the learning outcomes with the learners to best guarantee the highest level of application once they apply the knowledge or skill (Merriam & Leahy, 2005).

Assessment and Evaluation. As mentioned, assessment and evaluation are often thought of at the end of the instructional design process and at the end of the course or program. Assessments inform us to what extent the learners have mastered the new knowledge and skills. To take this a step further, consider this perspective—what if you also incorporate assessment during the course to proactively determine how what was learned will be applied in the learner's reality? In this light, assessment can be used as a tool to enhance learning transfer. Note that you cannot assess for application if you have not facilitated the practice of application during the learning process.

- Consider how you will assess the learning during the learning session and once the learner is applying the learning.
- Include planning for application outside of the classroom in assessment.
- If possible, assess after 2 weeks, 6 months, and 1 year, or simply ask learners to get back to you and let you know what they used and how.

Evaluation or feedback from the learners is also an important aspect. It provides the instructor and designer with feedback on the learning event. Were the learners comfortable and safe, was the instruction engaging and useful? This information can help us improve the learning environment and enhance the learning experience.

Learning Transfer: Selection of Methods and Resource Development. At this point in the design process, the designer has put a considerable amount of energy into determining who the learners are, what they need, and how to get there. The art of instruction is how to create a safe and positive learning environment—with a clear method of facilitation, providing ample resources—and help the learner move toward mastery of the intended outcomes. When developing or adopting the methods and learning resources to be used during instruction, consider the specific suggestions provided in each chapter:

- Chapter 1: General tools for transfer that may apply to the settings described in subsequent chapters
- Chapter 2: The integration of experiential learning techniques into instruction
- Chapter 3: Problem solving and the use of problem-based learning
- Chapter 4: Authenticity in the use of visuals, simulations, and technology
- Chapter 5: Safe and engaging environments and effective methods based on cognitive theory
- Chapter 6: Awareness of the potential effects of cultural or racial differences
- Chapter 7: Learning transfer as an implementation of personal change

For more information on instructional design, see *The Systematic Design of Instruction* (Dick, Carey, & Carey, 2009); *Instructional Design* (Smith & Ragan, 2005); *Principles of Instructional Design* (Gagne, Wager, Golas, & Keller, 2005); or *Survey of Instructional Development Models* (Gustafson & Branch, 2002).

The instructional designer spends the majority of the design process developing learning tools and identifying resources for instruction. Intentionally build in aspects that support transfer of learning. We will now continue with our own practice of learning transfer. We covered near transfer, not-so-near transfer, and farther transfer. Our final work is to consider an example of far transfer.

Far Transfer

As we continue through our practice of learning transfer, the highest form of transfer is applying the knowledge and skills to a completely different setting. To return to the apple pie example, I gained new knowledge and skills, transferred them from an apple pie to a peach pie, then even further to baking a large number of cupcakes. I can follow instructions; understand that things might vary, which affects outcome (temperature of oven, flavor of apples, varied level of juice in the fruit); and understand that I need to monitor the baking project or my dessert may be ruined. I can now apply this knowledge and skills to widely varied settings.

One skill you may have learned through this process is the concept of intentionality or purposefulness in planning. For each of you, where you can transfer or apply these skills may be different. An example is using intentionality for planning a community meeting. You start out by gaining information, such as when folks can come and where they would like to meet. What are your community members' interests and concerns? Then you select the venue and the dates and start to plan the activities based on desired outcomes. You will communicate the information and pay attention to all the details. Your new skill of intentionality in planning will help you create a community meeting that is effective and appreciated by everyone.

Conclusion

Throughout this issue, the authors provide guidance and examples to help you intentionally plan for learning transfer in your instructional activities. Transfer of learning is the goal for all learners, and it is our job as adult educators to take all the steps we can to ensure the highest probability of transfer. In this final chapter, we recommend that you follow the steps yourself to increase understanding and inclusion of methods and techniques that will enhance the likelihood of transfer for all your learners.

References

Baldwin, T. T., & Ford, J. K. (1988). Transfer of training: A review and direction for research. *Personnel Psychology, 41*, 63–105.

Broad, M. L. (1997). Transfer concepts and research overview. In M. L. Broad (Ed.), *Transferring learning to the workplace* (pp. 1–18). Alexandria, VA: American Society for Training and Development.

Dick, W., Carey, L., & Carey, J. O. (2009). *The systematic design of instruction*. Upper Saddle River, NJ: Pearson.

Ford, K. J., & Weissbein, D. A. (1997). Transfer of learning: An updated review and analysis. *Performance Improvement Quarterly, 10*(2), 22–41.

Gagne, R. M., Wager, W. W., Golas, K. C., & Keller, J. M. (2005). *Principles of instructional design* (5th ed). Belmont, CA: Wadsworth.

Gustafson, K. L., & Branch, R. M. (2002). *Survey of instructional development models* (4th ed). New York, NY: ERIC.

Holton, E. F., Bates, R. A., & Rouna, W. E. A. (2000). Development of a generalized learning transfer system inventory. *Human Resource Development Quarterly, 11*(4), 333–360.

Merriam, S. B., & Leahy, B. (2005). Learning transfer: A review of the research in adult education and training. *PAACE Journal of Lifelong Learning, 14*, 1–24.

Smith, P. L., & Ragan, T. J. (2005). *Instructional design* (3rd ed). Hoboken, NJ: Wiley.

KAREN KAMINSKI *is the chair of the Master of Education in Adult Education and Training in the School of Education at Colorado State University.*

JEFFREY M. FOLEY *is an assistant professor in the Adult Education and Training Program at Colorado State University.*

LEANN M. R. KAISER *is an assistant professor in the Adult Education and Training Program at Colorado State University.*

New Directions for Adult and Continuing Education • DOI: 10.1002/ace

INDEX

Page references followed by *fig* indicate an illustrated figure; followed by *t* indicate a table.

Active learning, 22*t*
Adams, D., 19
Adult basic education (ABE): how change is facilitated by, 72–74; intention for change explicit in, 71–72; the international and nonformal education context of, 64–65; learning transfer in the context of, 5–7, 13, 15; "polyrhythmic realities" on relevance of, 64
Adult educators: CDAI (Cultural Diversity Awareness Inventory) used with, 65; characteristics of brain-friendly learning, 55–57; encouraging repetition from multiple aspects, 12–13; how scaffolding is supported by, 9–10; implications of racial or cultural differences in learners for, 65–67; learning to emphasize personal change, 74–79; learning transaction as perceived by, 62–63; using PBL for facilitating learning transfer, 32–34; purposeful reflection encouraged by, 11–12; risk of learner misperception of racial or cultural adjustments by, 67; working with the learner's schema, 10–11. *See also* Learners
Affirmative action policies, 62
African American Leadership Program (CCL), 67
Ajzen, I., 77
Alessi, S. M., 40
Alfred, M., 64
Anderson, J. R., 27
Anderson, S. E., 74, 76
Armitage, C. J., 77, 78
Assessment: of instruction design for transfer, 85, 86–87; as type of reflective learning, 20
Asynchronous communication tools, 42–43
Atherton, J., 79, 80
Audience analysis, 84, 85–86
Authentic technology design: applied examples of, 45–46; for authenticity of interactivity, 44; for authenticity of representation or prototype, 43–44; of communication tools, 42–43; for

cueing task initiative, 42; in learning environment model, 41–42; to support authentic and appropriate feedback, 43; supporting authentic information, 44–45
Authenticity: accuracy, clarity, and completeness elements of, 41, 45; complex scaffolding focus on, 10; defining, 40–41; in designing technology to support learning transfer, 39–47; as problem-based learning characteristic, 31, 34; selecting components in design of technology, 41–45; understanding the complexity of, 39–40. *See also* Fidelity; Learning environment

Bailey, D. B., 75
Baldwin, T. T., 1, 62, 85
Bandura, A., 51, 53
Barnett, S. M., 24
Barrows, H. S., 31, 35
Bassok, M., 28, 32
Bastiaens, T., 40
Baszile, D., 66
Bates, R. A., 1, 86
Baumgartner, L. M., 71
Bayne, S., 40
Beach, K., 72, 73
Behavioral intention: beliefs and behavioral control impacting, 77–78; strength and implementation of, 78–79; Theory of planned behavior (TPB) on, 76–79
Beliefs: emotional reactions to challenged, 80; theory of planned behavior (TPB) on learner's intentions due to, 76–79; when learners resist change due to their, 79–80
Benander, R., 8
Bereiter, C., 41
Blacks: comparing median household net work of Whites, Hispanics, and, 62; comparing unemployment of Whites, Hispanics, and, 62. *See also* Racial or cultural differences
Bloom, B. S., 28
Bloom's taxonomy, 12

Bonk, C., 19
Bosch, M. C., 74
Boyd, E. M., 19
Brain: comparing neuron that has been trained vs. not trained, 50*fig*; designing instruction compatible with processes of the, 49–51; how fear and pleasure communicate in the, 53; role of stress and threat in learning processes of the, 53–54
Brain stem, 53
Brain-friendly learning facilitators: attitude and listening skills of, 56–57; preparation by, 55–56
Brain-friendly learning teaching: addressing stress-threat balance to create, 53–54; characteristics of facilitators that use, 55–57; creating an enriched environment for, 51–55; learning benefits of a, 51; learning communities as, 20, 52; learning transfer through, 49–51, 57–58; role of emotions in creating, 52–53; types of methods used for, 54–55
Branch, R. M., 85, 87
Bringle, R. G., 19
Broad, M. L., 1, 6, 86
Brookfield, S., 71, 79
Brown v. Board of Education, 62

Caffarella, R. S., 61, 64, 65, 71
Calais, G. J., 6, 7, 8
Carey, J. O., 86, 87
Carey, L., 86, 87
Case-structured curriculum, 31, 33
Casper, E. S., 77
Catching, C., 67
CDAI (Cultural Diversity Awareness Inventory), 65
CDW-G (2012), 13
Ceci, S. J., 24
Center for Creative Leadership (CCL), 65, 67
Center for Creative Leadership (CCL) African American Leadership Program, 67
Change: adult education facilitation of, 72–74; adult education programs and explicit intention for, 71–72; concerns-based adoption model (CBAM) of, 74–76; consequential transition type of, 73; encouraging adult educators' to focus on personal, 74–79;

literature on transformative learning focused on, 71; theory of planned behavior (TPB) on, 76–79; when learners resist, 79–80. *See also* Knowledge application
Chrobot-Mason, D., 63
Civil Rights Act (1964), 62
Clark, R. E., 30
Clément, E., 29
Closson, R., 2, 61, 64, 67, 69
Cognitive theory: applied to how the brain learns, 49–50*fig*; relationship between learning transfer and, 49–51
"Collateral" consequential transition, 73
Columbia University, 63
Coming-to-presence activity, 54
Communication: designing technological tools of, 42–43; facilitator's listening skills for, 56–57
Communication technology tools: designing authentic, 42–43; synchronous and asynchronous, 42–43
Community learning, 10
Concept mapping: description of, 13; key elements of, 13, 14*fig*
Concerns-based adoption model (CBAM): assumptions and stages of concern of, 74–75*t*; conceptualization of change by, 74; on implementation of change, 76; on levels of use based on change, 75*t*–76
Conner, M., 77, 78
Consequential transition: "collateral transition" type of, 73; "encompassing transition" type of, 73
Content. *See* Curriculum
Continuing education vegetable gardening course, 23–24
Cooperative learning: description of, 18, 19; ESL course inclusion of, 22; vegetable gardening course use of, 24
Cormier, S. M., 1
Cox, B., 20
Cozolino, L., 51, 52, 53, 54
Cranton, P., 20, 55, 71
Cultural differences. *See* Racial or cultural differences
Cunningham, D. J., 19
Curriculum: organized from immediately to remotely applicable contexts, 35; PBL as problem- or case-organized, 31, 33; problems used in, 30, 31, 33, 34–35; racial and cultural differences

considered in the, 65–67. *See also* Instruction

Daloz, L. A., 53, 57
Decontextualized learning environment, 29–30
Detterman, D. K., 7
Dewey, J., 18
Diamond, M., 51
Dick, W., 86, 87
Dochy, F., 34
Doyle, S., 7
Dufresne, T., 79

Eccles, M. P., 74
Emotions: critical role in learning played by, 52–53; how fear and pleasure communicate in the brain, 53; making learning environment emotionally safe and fear of negative, 53; reactions to challenged beliefs, 80; stress and threatening, 53–54
"Encompassing" consequential transition, 73
Engeström, Y., 81
English as a Second Language (ESL) courses: application of learning transfer of, 6; experiential learning techniques for, 22–23
Evaluation of instruction, 85, 86–87. *See also* Feedback
Evenson, D. H., 34
Experiential learning techniques: cooperative learning, 18, 19, 22, 24; description of, 17; integrating, 21–24; learning transfer aligned to, 20–21, 22t, 24–25; National Outdoor Leadership School (NOLS) use of, 21; problem-based learning, 18, 23–24, 27–36, 66; project-based learning, 18, 23; reflective learning, 19–20, 23, 32, 33–34, 36; service learning, 19, 22–23. *See also* Learning

Facilitators. *See* Adult educators
Fales, A. M., 19
Far transfer: comparing application of near and, 28–29; description of, 7, 28, 88
Farther transfer, 84
Fear and pleasure, 53
Feedback: CCI's African American Leadership program use of, 67; on instruction design for transfer, 85, 86–87; learning

transfer improved through quality, 20; medical training technology providing authentic, 46; technology design to support authentic and appropriate, 43. *See also* Evaluation of instruction
Fenwick, T. J., 18
Fidelity, 40. *See also* Authenticity
Fight, freeze, or flee response, 53
Foley, J. M., 1, 2, 3, 5, 15, 83, 89
Ford, J. K., 1, 9, 62, 88
Ford, K. J., 1, 86
Foundational knowledge: as barrier to learning transfer, 8; schema theory on new information processed using, 50
Frontczak, N. T., 20
Fry, R., 62
Furman, N., 1, 17, 18, 20, 26

Gagne, R. M., 87
Galef, B., 50
Gallagher, S. A., 34
Genereux, R., 27
Gick, M. L., 28
Gijbels, D., 34
Given, B., 52
Golas, K. C., 87
Gollwitzer, P. M., 78, 79
Gookin, J., 20
Grol, R.P.T.M., 74
Group processing and reflection, 19
"Guesstimating," 73
Gulikers, J., 40
Gunn, A., 49, 56
Gupta, T. S., 35
Gustafson, K. L., 85, 87
Guy, T., 64–65

Haas, C., 18
Hager, P., 9, 72
Hagman, J. D., 1
Hall, G. E., 75
Hamm, M., 19
Haney Lopez, I., 62
Hardré, P. L., 2, 39, 47
Harlow, R., 62
Haskell, E. H., 8
Haskell's taxonomies for transfer of learning, 7–8
Hatcher, J. A., 19
Hawley, W., 58
Hays, R., 35
Healthy Memory Company Ltd., 50

Helplessness, 54
Herrington, J., 40
High-road learning transfer, 7
Hispanics: comparing median household
    net work of Whites, Blacks, and, 62;
    comparing unemployment of Whites,
    Blacks, and, 62. See also Racial or cul-
    tural differences
Hmelo-Silver, C. E., 31, 34
Hodgldns, S., 78
Hodkinson, P., 9, 72
Hoge, P., 51
Holder, E., 67
Holton, E. F., 1, 86
Holyoak, K. J., 28, 32
Hopson, J., 51
Household net work (racial differences),
    62
Hulscher, M.E.J.L., 74
Hung, W., 2, 27, 28, 29, 31, 32, 34, 35,
    38

Ill-structured problems, 30, 31
Illeris, K., 8, 9
Instruction: brain-friendly learning teach-
    ing, 20, 49–58; concept mapping used
    for, 13, 14fig; for creating brain-friendly
    learning environment, 54–55; decon-
    textualized learning environments of
    traditional, 29–30; how learner's
    schema impacts, 10–11; using meta-
    phors as part of, 57–58fig; problem-
    based learning (PBL), 18, 23–24,
    27–39, 66; purposeful reflection fol-
    lowing, 11–12; racial and cultural dif-
    ferences considered in content and,
    65–67; repetition from multiple
    aspects, 12–13; scaffolding, 9–10; tra-
    ditional use of abstract forms of knowl-
    edge in, 29. See also Curriculum;
    Learning transaction; Learning transfer
Instruction design: assessment and evalu-
    ation, 85, 86–87; audience analysis for,
    84, 85–86; for far transfer, 88; for far-
    ther transfer, 84; integrating multitude
    of delivery methods into, 13; intention-
    ally building transfer in instructional
    design for, 84–88; learning outcomes
    and, 85, 86; for near transfer, 83–84;
    needs assessment for, 84, 85; for not-so-
    near transfer, 84; racial and cultural dif-
    ferences considerations for, 65–67;
    repetition from multiple aspects built

into, 12–13; selection of methods and
    resource development, 87–88; stake-
    holder input and buy-in for, 74, 85
Instructional Design (Smith and Ragan), 87

Jonassen, D. H., 29, 30, 31, 32
Jordi, R., 20

Kahnweiler, W. M., 20
Kaiser, L.M.R., 1, 2, 3, 5, 15, 83, 89
Kaminski, K., 2, 3, 49, 59, 83, 89
Kaye, S., 64, 67
Keller, J. M., 87
Kirschner, P. A., 30, 40
Klampfleitner, M., 40
Knottenbelt, M., 40
Knowledge: prior or foundational, 8, 50;
    situational, 29–30; traditional instruc-
    tion using abstract forms of, 29
Knowledge application: comparing far
    and near transfer, 28–29, 83–84; of
    continuing education vegetable garden-
    ing course, 23–24; of ESL course, 6,
    22–23; experiential learning techniques
    for, 22–24; obstacles to learning trans-
    fer and, 8–9, 29–30; of online personal
    finance course, 23. See also Change;
    Learning transfer
Kochhar, R., 62
Konrad, A. M., 63
Kovalik, S., 51
Kramer, E., 8
Kreber, C., 40
Kulik, C. T., 63

Lamont, A. C., 50
Language-learning technology, 46
Leahy, B., 1, 6, 84, 86
Learners: allowing team choice and com-
    mon interests by, 20; audience analysis
    of, 84, 85–86; lack of support structure
    by underresourced, 57; learning trans-
    action as perceived by, 63; learning
    transfer influenced by racial and cul-
    tural differences of, 61–67; learning
    transfer role of characteristics of, 61;
    leveraging experiential learning tech-
    niques for, 17–25; McClusky's theory of
    margin on, 56–57; obstacles to learning
    transfer faced by, 8–9, 29–30; PBL
    encouragement of metacognition
    through reflection by, 36; promote abil-
    ity to ask effective questions during

PBL instruction, 35–36; purposeful reflection by, 11–12; scaffolding of learning by, 9–10; schemas held by, 10–11; Theory of planned behavior (TBP) on behavioral intention of, 76–79; when they resist change, 79–80. *See also* Adult educators

Learning: accommodative, 8–9, 79; assimilative, 8–9, 79; cooperative, 18, 19, 22, 24; cumulative, 8–9; Piaget's assimilative and accommodative divisions of, 79; problem-based, 18, 23–24, 27–36, 66; project-based, 18, 23; reflective, 19–20, 23, 32, 33–34; role of emotions in process of, 52–53; self-directed, 31–32, 33, 35; service, 19, 22–23; transformative, 8–9, 71–80. *See also* Experiential learning techniques

Learning in Adulthood (Merriam, Caffarella, and Baumgartner), 71

Learning communities: creating an enriched learning environment through, 52; as form of learning environment, 20

Learning environment: authenticity of the, 41–42; brain-friendly, 51–57; decontextualized, 29–30; learning obstacles of traditional, 29–30; making them emotionally safe, 53; PBL encouragement of metacognition through reflective activities, 36; promote ability to ask effective questions during PBL, 35–36; self-directed learning encouraged by, 31–32, 33, 35. *See also* Authenticity

Learning outcomes, 85, 86

Learning transaction: adult educator's perception of the, 62–63; content and context of the, 63; examining the individual elements of the, 62; how racial or cultural differences may influence the, 62–63; learner's perception of the, 63. *See also* Instruction

Learning transfer: adult education context of, 5–7, 13, 15; authenticity in designing technology to support, 39–47; barriers to, 8–9; brain-friendly instruction and, 49–58; definition of, 6, 17, 27–28, 49; far, 7, 28, 88; intentionally built into design of instruction, 84–88; learner characteristics as key factor in, 61; leveraging experiential learning techniques for, 17–25; models of, 7–8; near, 7, 28, 83–84; PBL for facilitating, 18, 23–24, 27–36, 66; racial and cul-

tural factors to consider in, 61–67; workplace as primary site of research on, 6. *See also* Instruction; Knowledge application

Learning transfer barriers: common classroom practices as, 8; lack of foundational knowledge as, 8, 50; learning space boundaries as, 8–9; traditional use of abstract forms knowledge as, 29

Learning transfer levels: far transfer, 7, 28, 88; high- and low-road, 7; knowledge application, 6, 8–9, 22–24, 29–30, 83–84; near transfer, 7, 28, 83–84; negative and positive, 7

Learning transfer models: Haskell's taxonomies for transfer of learning, 7–8; high- and low-road transfer, 7; near and far transfer, 7; positive and negative transfer, 7

Learning transfer tools: concept mapping, 13, 14*fig*; diversity of delivery methods, 13; instructional design and selection of, 87–88; purposeful reflection, 11–12; quality feedback as, 20; repetition from multiple aspects, 12–13; scaffolding, 9–10; schema, 10–11

Leberman, S., 7

Lecoutre, B., 29

Lecoutre, M.-P., 29

LeDoux, J., 53

Lee, C. D., 20

Lemme, B. H., 79

Lightner, R., 8

Limbic system, 53

Linnehan, F., 63

Listening skills, 56

Liu, R., 31, 32

Loucks, S. F., 75

Low-road learning transfer, 7

Lupart, J., 17

McClusky, H. Y., 56

McClusky's theory of margin, 56–57

McCune, V., 40

McDonald, L., 7

McGinty, J., 2, 49, 59

McKeachie, W., 50, 54, 58

McKeough, A., 17

Marienau, C., 18

Marini, A., 17, 27

Martin, L., 64

Mayer, R., 20

Medical training technology, 46

Merriam, S. B., 1, 6, 71, 84, 86

Metacognition: brain-friendly teaching that supports, 55; problem-based learning opportunities for, 36

Metaphors: example of using, 58*fig*; instruction using, 57–58

Mezirow, J., 56

Motivation: concerns-based adoption model (CBAM) on change, 74–76; theory of planned behavior (TPB) on learner's intentions and, 76–79

Multiple viewpoints: instruction using repetition from, 12–13; reflective learning using, 20

National Outdoor Leadership School (NOLS), 21

Near transfer: comparing application of far and, 28–29, 88; description of, 7, 28, 83–84; not-so-near, 84

Needs assessment, 84, 85

Negative learning transfer, 7

Neurons (trained vs. not trained), 50*fig*

Nielsen, M., 50

Norman, G. R., 31

Not-so-near transfer, 84

Ohlott, P., 65

Oliver, R., 40

Olsen, K., 51

Online personal finance course, 23

Orbeil, S., 78

Packer, M., 24

Paisley, K., 20

Palmer, P. J., 12

Palsha, S. A., 75

Patton, L., 67

Pepper, M. B., 63

Perceived threats, 53

Perkins, D. N., 7, 28

Pew Research Center, 62

Piaget, J., 18, 79

Pleasure and fear, 53

"Polyrhythmic realities," 64

Positive learning transfer, 7

Pratt, D., 62

Principles of Instructional Design (Gagne, Wager, Golas, and Keller), 87

Prior knowledge: learning transfer blocked by lack of, 8; schema theory on new information processed using, 50

Problem-based learning instruction: barriers to knowledge application in traditional, 29–30; characteristics of, 31–32; design guidelines for effective, 34–36; promote ability to ask effective questions during, 35–36; using self-directed learning, 31–32, 33, 35; well-structured vs. ill-structured problems used in, 30, 31

Problem-based learning (PBL): description of, 18, 31; for facilitating learning transfer, 32–34; instruction of, 29–36; learning transfer barriers in traditional, 29–30; online personal finance course using, 23; racial and cultural differences considered in, 66; scaffolding pertaining to, 10; self-directed learning element of, 31–32, 33, 35; vegetable gardening course use of, 23–24; well-structured vs. ill-structured problems used in, 30, 31

Problems: using authentic, 31, 34; using contextually meaningful, 34; embedding profession specifics and culture in, 34–35; how the brain seeks novel way to solve complex, 50; ill-structured, 30, 31; problem-based learning curriculum organized around, 31, 33

Project-based learning: description of, 18; online personal finance course using, 23; vegetable gardening course use of, 23

Purposeful reflection, 11–12

Racial or cultural differences: affirmative action policies on, 62; CCL's African American Leadership program use of feedback on, 67; CDAI (Cultural Diversity Awareness Inventory) to assess awareness of, 65; examining how they may impact learning transfer, 61–62; how they may influence the learning transaction, 62–63; implications for adult educators and course content, 65–67; risk of learner misperception of educator adjustments for, 67; theoretical and anecdotal evidence for learning transfer influencing, 63–65; in unemployment and household net worth, 62. *See also* Blacks; Hispanics; Whites

Radin, J., 2, 49, 59

Ratey, J., 53